Mathcounts Chapter Practice

http://www.mymathcounts.com/index.php

This book can be used by 6th to 8th grade students preparing for Mathcounts Chapter and State Competitions.

This book contains a collection of five sets of practice tests for MATHCOUNTS Chapter (Regional) competitions, including Sprint and Target rounds. One or more detailed solutions are included for every problem.

We would also like to thank the following people who kindly reviewed the manuscripts and made valuable suggestions and corrections: Kevin Yang (IA), Skyler Wu (CA), Reece Yang (IA), Kelly Li (IL), Geoffrey Ding (IL), Raymond Suo (KY), Sreeni Bajji (MI), Yashwanth Bajji (MI), Ying Peng, Ph.D (MN), Eric Lu (NC), Akshra Paimagam (NC), Sean Jung (NC), Melody Wen (NC), Esha Agarwal (NC), Jason Gu (NJ), Daniel Ma (NY), Yiqing Shen (TN), Chris Kan (VA), Evan Ling (VA), Tristan Ma (VA), and Lizzie Zhou (VA).

Please email us at mymathcounts@gmail.com if you see any typos or mistakes or you have a different solution to any of the problems in the book. We really appreciate your help in improving the book.

Copyright © 2015 by mymathcounts.com. All rights reserved. Printed in the United States of America. Reproduction of any portion of this book without the written permission of the authors is strictly prohibited, except as may be expressly permitted by the U.S. Copyright Act.

ISBN-13: 978-1508662051
ISBN-10: 1508662053
BISAC: Education / Teaching Methods & Materials / Mathematics

TABLE OF CONTENTS

1. Mathcounts Chapter Competition Practice Test 1   1
   - Sprint Round   1
   - Target Round   8
   - Answer keys   13
   - Solutions   14

2. Mathcounts Chapter Competition Practice Test 2   28
   - Sprint Round   28
   - Target Round   34
   - Answer keys   39
   - Solutions   40

3. Mathcounts Chapter Competition Practice Test 3   54
   - Sprint Round   54
   - Target Round   60
   - Answer keys   65
   - Solutions   66

4. Mathcounts Chapter Competition Practice Test 4   80
   - Sprint Round   80
   - Target Round   86
   - Answer keys   91
   - Solutions   92

5. Mathcounts Chapter Competition Practice Test 5   106
   - Sprint Round   106
   - Target Round   114
   - Answer keys   119
   - Solutions   120

Index   136

This page is intentionally left blank.

Mathcounts Chapter Competition Practice   Test 1

MATHCOUNTS

■ **Chapter Competition** ■
Practice Test 1
Sprint Round Problems 1–30

Name _____

DO NOT BEGIN UNTIL YOU ARE INSTRUCTED TO DO SO.

This round of the competition consists of 30 problems. You will have 40 minutes to complete the problems. You are not allowed to use calculators, books or any other aids during this round. If you are wearing a calculator wrist watch, please give it to your proctor now. Calculations may be done on scratch paper. All answers must be complete, legible and simplified to lowest terms. Record only final answers in the blanks in the right-hand column of the competition booklet. If you complete the problems before time is called, use the remaining time to check your answers.

Total Correct	Scorer's Initials

Mathcounts Chapter Competition Practice   Test 1

1. Calculate: $9 \times 8 \div 9 \times 8$.

2. The pie chart shown represents a survey of East Carolinians who do not use the Internet. What is the percent of East Carolinians non-users for whom cost and time are *not* the primary barrier?

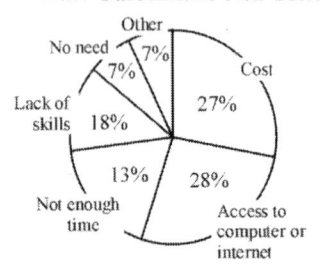

   Primary Barrier to Internet Access
   East Carolinians Non-Users
   - Other 7%
   - No need 7%
   - Cost 27%
   - Lack of skills 18%
   - Not enough time 13%
   - Access to computer or internet 28%

3. It is now 12:00:00 midnight, as read on a 12-hour digital clock. In 2016 hours, 20 minutes and 16 seconds the time will be $A : B : C$. What is the value of $A + B + C$?

4. Shooting hoops for 15 minutes burns 75 calories. How many calories would Kerry burn shooting hoops if he shot hoops 45 minutes every day for one month in February, 2016?

5. An ant crawls along the edge of a regular hexagon from the vertex A clock wisely. How far is the ant from the vertex A after it craws 2016 inches? Each edge of the hexagon is 32 inches.

Mathcounts Chapter Competition Practice   **Test 1**

6. Four times the product of three consecutive positive integers is 2016. What is the sum of the three positive integers?

7. The ratio of the number of dollars Alex has to the number of dollars Bob has is 3 : 4. After Alex gives $40 to Bob, the ratio of the number of dollars Alex has to the number of dollars Bob becomes 1 : 3. How many dollars does Alex have at first?

8. An escalator moves up at a constant speed. If Alex walks up the escalator at the rate 120 steps per minute, he reaches the top in 30 seconds. If he walks up the escalator at the rate 80 steps per minute, he reaches the top in 40 seconds. How many steps does the escalator have?

9. Ross has ten boxes. Seven of the boxes contain pencils, five of the boxes contain pens, and four of the boxes contain both pens and pencils. How many boxes contain neither pens nor pencils?

10. How many combinations of pennies, nickels and/or dimes are there with a total value of 35¢?

11. What is the value of the following expression:
$1 - 3 + 5 - 7 + 9 - 11 + ... - 2015 + 2017$?

12. A rectangular tile measures 4 inches by 5 inches. What is the fewest number of these tiles that are needed to completely cover a rectangular region that is 5 feet by 8 feet?

13. When plotted in the standard rectangular coordinate system, quadrilateral $ABCD$ has vertices $A(2, 5)$, $B(4, 1)$, and $C(1, -3)$ and $D(-1, 1)$. What is the area of quadrilateral $ABCD$?

14. Betsy receives a 15% commission on every sale she makes. On the sale of a $150 calculator (before any discounts), how many more dollars will she receive if her commission is based on the original price of the calculator rather than the price of the calculator after a 40% discount?

15. Five distinct points A, B, C, D and E lie on a line, but not necessarily in that order. Use the information below to determine the number of units in the length of segment BE.
    - B is the midpoint of segment AD.
    - C is the midpoint of segment BD.
    - Both E and B are the same distance from D.
    - The distance from A to B is 6 units.

16. Alex paid $945 to transport his animals by ferry. The costs were $3, $2 and $1 for each cats, dog, and squirrel, respectively. The ratio of cats to dogs was 2 : 9, and dog to squirrel 3 : 7. How many cats were there?

17. What is the sum of all the positive two-digit integers with 12 factors ?

18. The points $A(-4, 3)$, $B(-3, 6)$ and $C(0, 3)$ are plotted in the standard rectangular coordinate system to form triangle ABC. Triangle ABC is translated five units to the right and two units downward to triangle $A'B'C'$, in such a way that A' is the image of A, B' is the image of B, and C' is the image of C. What is the midpoint of segment $A'C'$? Express your answer as an ordered pair.

19. The positive difference of the cube of an integer and the square of the same integer is 1210. Find the integer.

20. A rectangular sheet of paper is folded three times and then cut, as shown below. All fold lines are dashed, and the portion that is to be cut away is shaded.

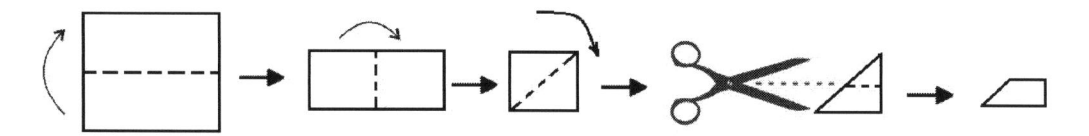

Mathcounts Chapter Competition Practice   **Test 1**

Which of the following drawings (*B, C, D,* or *E*) shows what the paper looks like when it is unfolded after the cuts?

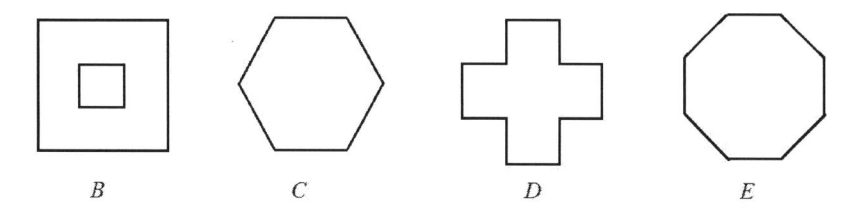

       B   C   D   E

21. The average value of four distinct positive integers *a, b, c,* and *d* is 18. If $b - a = 7$, and $d - c = 11$, find the greatest possible value of *d*. It is known that $a < b < c < d$.

22. How many 4-digit positive integers divisible by 15 can be formed by using the digits 0, 2, 4, 6, and 9? No digit is repeated in any of the 4-digit integers.

23. Zack has created this rule for generating sequences of whole numbers.
     If a number is less than 45, triple the number.
     If a number is 45 or more, subtract 30 from it.
For example, if Zack starts with 12, he gets the sequence 36, 108, 78, 48, 18, ... If the third number in Zack's sequence is 45, what is the sum of the four distinct numbers that could have been the first number in his sequence?

24. Reverse the two digits of my age, divide by four, add 9, and the result is my age. How many years old am I?

25. The sequence of integers in the row of squares and in each of the two columns of squares form three distinct arithmetic sequences. What is the value of *x*?

5

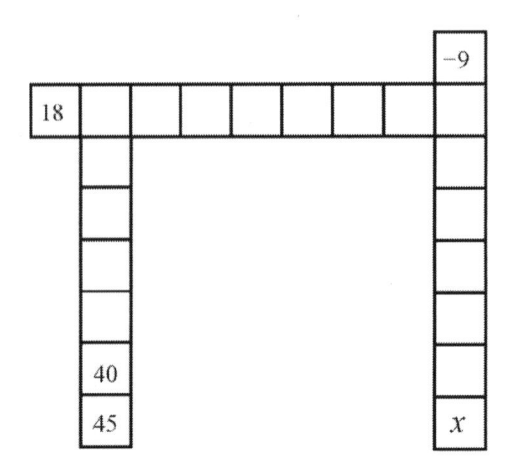

26. In the figure shown, a circle passes through two adjacent vertices of a rectangle *ABCD* (with $AB = 3\sqrt{3}$, and $AD = 6$) and is tangent to the opposite side of the rectangle. What is the area of the circle? Express your answer in terms of π.

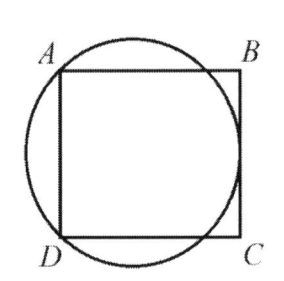

27. The function *f* is defined by $f(n) = f(n-1) + 2f(n-2)$. It is also true that $f(1) = 20$ and $f(3) = 16$. What is the value of $f(6)$?

28. If $x + \dfrac{1}{y} = y + \dfrac{1}{z} = z + \dfrac{1}{x}$, where *x*, *y*, and *z* are distinct real numbers, what is the positive value of the product *xyz*?

29. David has ten sticks measuring 1 cm, 2 cm, 3 cm, 4 cm, 5 cm, 6 cm, 7 cm, 8 cm, 9 cm, and 10 cm. Using at most two sticks in any one side of a square, how many squares are possible if the sticks are joined only at their endpoints?

Mathcounts Chapter Competition Practice   Test 1

30. As shown in the figure, *AE* and *BF* cut the rectangle *ABCD* into 4 regions. The area of △*EFG* is 4 cm². The area of △*ABG* is 9 cm². The area of quadrilateral *ADFG* is 10 cm². Find the area of quadrilateral *BCEG*.

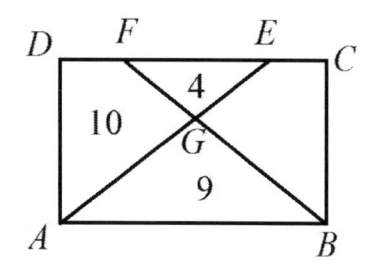

MATHCOUNTS

■ **Chapter Competition**
Practice Test 1
Target Round Problems ■

Name _____

DO NOT BEGIN UNTIL YOU ARE INSTRUCTED TO DO SO.

This round of the competition consists of eight problems, which will be presented in pairs. Work on one pair of problems will be completed and answers will be collected before the next pair is distributed. The time limit for each pair of problems is six minutes. The first pair of problems is on the other side of this sheet. When told to do so, turn the page over and begin working. Record your final answer in the designated space on the problem sheet. All answers must be complete, legible and simplified to lowest terms. This round assumes the use of calculators, and calculations may also be done on scratch paper, but no other aids are allowed.

Total Correct	Scorer's Initials

Mathcounts Chapter Competition Practice   Test 1

1. If $\dfrac{x}{7}$ is a proper fraction, and the sum of the digits beyond the decimal point in the decimal representation of $\dfrac{x}{7}$ is 2017, what is the sum of all possible values of x?

2. When the three integers 189, 139, and 99 are divided by a positive integer d, where $d > 1$, the sum of the remainders is 50. What is the possible value of d?

Mathcounts Chapter Competition Practice   **Test 1**

3. Alex ordered online 5 pounds of oranges and paid $32.35. The fruit was marked 90% of water content when it was shipped. When the package arrived at his home, the measured water content was 80%. What was the actual price per pound did Alex pay for the oranges? Express your answer as the nearest dollar.

4. The symbols ◯, △, ◇, and ⬡ represent four different integers. The number under each figure represents the sum of the numbers represented by the three figures. What is the value for x?

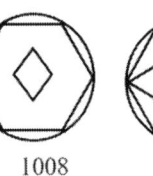

    1007   1008   2015   2018 x

10

5. Find the greatest whole number that MUST be a factor of the sum of any six consecutive positive odd numbers.

6. Figure 1 is formed by four congruent regular hexagons of side length of 2. Three vertices are connected to form triangle ABC (Figure 2). What is the area of triangle ABC? Express your answer in simplest radical form.

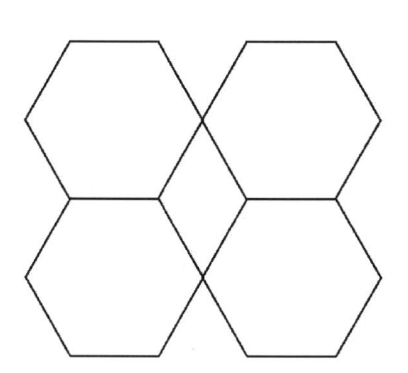

Figure 1

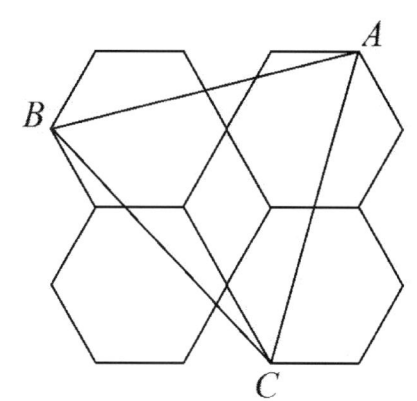

Figure 2

Mathcounts Chapter Competition Practice   **Test 1**

7. Alex and Bob were two men having a meal. Alex brought 3 loaves of bread, and Bob brought 2. These loaves of bread are identical. A third man, Charles, came and joined them. They together ate the whole 5 loaves. As Charles left, he paid $20. How many dollars should Alex get?

8. Anna whispers her birth month to Bob, and birth date to Chris. The boys don't know one another's numbers but they do know that the all possible birth dates are as follows:

    5/17
    6/14   6/15
    7/11   7/12
    8/11   8/12   8/14

    Chris says, "I know when Anna's birthday is"!

    Then Bob says, "At first, I didn't know when Anna's birthday was, but I know now".

    When is Anna's birthday?

Mathcounts Chapter Competition Practice — Test 1

ANSWER KEYS TO TEST 1

SPRINT ROUND

1. 64.
2. 60%.
3. 48.
4. 6525.
5. 64.
6. 24.
7. $ 96.
8. 80.
9. 2.
10. 20.
11. 1009.
12. 288.
13. 20.
14. 9.
15. 12.
16. 42.
17. 402.
18. (3, 1).
19. 11.
20. D.
21. 37.
22. 12.
23. 180.
24. 27.
25. 12.
26. 12π.
27. -64.
28. 1.
29. 19.
30. 7 cm^2.

TARGET ROUND

1. 7.
2. 29.
3. 13.
4. 2016.
5. 12.
6. $13\sqrt{3}$.
7. 16.
8. 6/15.

Mathcounts Chapter Competition Practice   Test 1

SPRINT ROUND SOLUTIONS TO TEST 1

1. Solution: 64.
$9 \times 8 \div 9 \times 8 = 9 \div 9 \times 8 \times 8 = 64$.

2. Solution: 60%.
The percent of East Carolinians non-users for whom cost is the primary barrier: 27%.
The percent of East Carolinians non-users for whom time is the primary barrier: 13%.
The percent of East Carolinians non-users for whom cost and time are *not* the primary barrier: 1 – 27% - 13% = 60%.

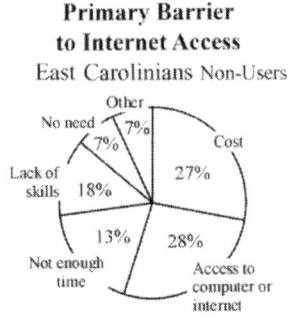

Primary Barrier to Internet Access
East Carolinians Non-Users
- Other 7%
- No need 7%
- Cost 27%
- Lack of skills 18%
- Not enough time 13%
- Access to computer or internet 28%

3. Solution: 48.
It is 12:00:00 noon.
$2016 = 24 \times 84 = 84$ days. In 2016 hours, the time will still be 12:00:00 noon.
In 2016 hours 20 minutes and 16 seconds, the clock will show 12: 20:16. Therefore, the value of $A + B + C = 12 + 20 + 16 = 48$.

4. Solution: 6525.
Kerry burns $\frac{45}{15} \times 75 = 225$ calories every day. 2016 is a leap year since 2016 is divisible by 4. So February, 2016 has 29 days. The answer is $29 \times 225 = 6525$.

5. Solution: 64.
$2016 = 6 \times 32 \times 10 + 96$.

The ant will be back to the vertex A after 10 rounds. $96 = 32 + 32 + 32$. So the ant is located at vertex C. Since the hexagon is regular, $AB = AD = DC$. So the distance from A to C is $32 + 32 = 64$ inches.

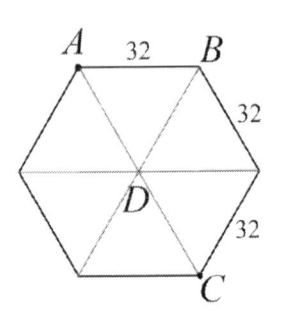

6. Solution: 24.
Let the three consecutive integers be $(x – 1)$, x, and $(x + 1)$.

14

Mathcounts Chapter Competition Practice   Test 1

We have $4(x-1) x (x+1) = 2016$ $\Rightarrow$ $(x-1) x (x+1) = 504 = 2^3 \times 3^2 \times 7 = 7 \times 8 \times 9$.
$(x-1) + x + (x+1) = 7 + 8 + 9 = 24$.

7. Solution: $ 96.
Method 1:
Let x be the sum of their money. x does not change during the process. The fraction of Alex's money at first is $\frac{3}{3+4}$. The fraction of Alex's money after is $\frac{1}{1+3}$.

$\frac{3}{3+4} x - \frac{1}{1+3} x = 540$ $\Rightarrow$ $x = \$224$.

$\frac{3}{3+4} x = \frac{3}{7} \times 224 = \$96$.

Method 2:
Let x be the Alex's money and y be Bob's money originally.

$\frac{x}{y} = \frac{3}{4}$ $\Rightarrow$ $y = \frac{4}{3} x$ (1)

$\frac{x-40}{y+40} = \frac{1}{3}$ $\Rightarrow$ $3(x-40) = y + 40$ (2)

Substituting (1) into (2): $3x - 120 = \frac{4}{3} x + 40$ $\Rightarrow$ $3x - \frac{4}{3} x = 40 + 120$ $\Rightarrow$ $\frac{5}{3} x = 160$
$\Rightarrow x = 96$.

8. Solution: 80.
Let x be the speed of the escalator in steps per minute.
$\frac{30}{60}(120 + x) = \frac{40}{60}(80 + x)$ $\Rightarrow$ $\frac{1}{2}(120 + x) = \frac{2}{3}(80 + x)$ $\Rightarrow$ $3(120 + x) = 4(80 + x)$
$\Rightarrow 360 + 3x = 320 + 4x$ $\Rightarrow x = 40$.

The number of steps of the escalator is $\frac{30}{60}(120 + x) = \frac{1}{2}(120 + 40) = 80$.

9. Solution: 2.
Let x be the boxes contain neither pens nor pencils.

Mathcounts Chapter Competition Practice Test 1

By two events formula of PIE (Principle of Inclusion and Exclusion), $10 - x = 7 + 5 - 4$
$\Rightarrow \quad 10 - x = 8 \quad \Rightarrow \quad x = 2.$

10. Solution: 20.
Let p, n, and d be the number of pennies, nickels, and dimes.

$p + 5n + 10d = 35$ (1)
At most d can be 3.
Case 1: When $d = 3$, (1) becomes $p + 5n = 5$. When $p = 0$, $n = 1$; when $p = 5$, $n = 0$.

Case 2: When $d = 2$, (1) becomes $p + 5n = 15$. When $p = 0$, $n = 3$; when $p = 5$, $n = 2$; when $p = 10$, $n = 1$; when $p = 15$, $n = 0$.

Case 3: When $d = 1$, (1) becomes $p + 5n = 25$. p can be 0, 5, 10, 15, 20, 25 and the corresponding values of n are 5, 4, 3, 2, 1, and 0.

Case 4: When $d = 0$, (1) becomes $p + 5n = 35$. p can be 0, 5, 10, 15, 20, 25, 30, and 35. The corresponding values of n are 7, 6, 5, 4, 3, 2, 1, and 0.

The answer is $2 + 4 + 6 + 8 = 20$.

11. Solution: 1,009.
Let n be the number of terms from 1 to 2015.
$2015 = 1 + (n - 1) \times 2 \quad \Rightarrow n = 1008.$
When we group the numbers by pairs, we get $1008 \div 2 = 504$ pairs.
So $(1 - 3) + (5 - 7) + (7 - 9) + 11 - \ldots 2013 - 2015 = -2 \times 504 = -1008.$
The answer is $(1 - 3) + (5 - 7) + (7 - 9) + \ldots + (2013 - 2015) + 2017 = -1008 + 2017 = 1,009.$

12. Solution: 288.

$\dfrac{(5 \times 12)}{5} \times \dfrac{(8 \times 12)}{4} = 12 \times 24 = 288.$

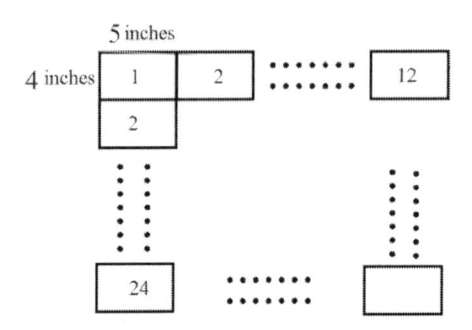

16

Mathcounts Chapter Competition Practice   Test 1

13. Solution: 20.

Method 1:
By the shoelace formula, the area is

$$A = \frac{1}{2} \begin{vmatrix} 2 & 5 \\ 4 & 1 \\ 1 & -3 \\ -1 & 1 \\ 2 & 5 \end{vmatrix}$$

$= \frac{1}{2} \times |2 - 12 + 1 - 5 - (2 + 3 + 1 + 20)|$

$= \frac{1}{2} \times |-40| = 20$.

Method 2:

$5 \times 8 - 3 \times 4/2 - 4 \times 2/2 - 2 \times 4/2 - 3 \times 4/2 = 20$.

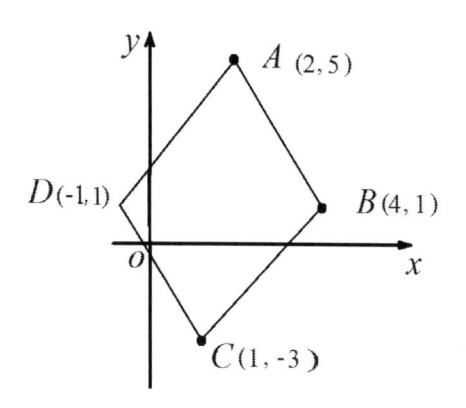

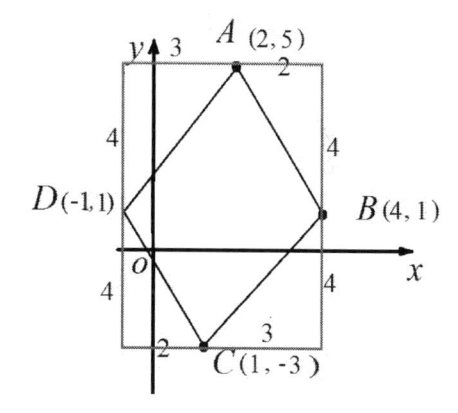

14. Solution: 9.
Betsy receives $0.15 \times 150 = \$22.5$ commission before discount.
Betsy receives $0.15 \times (150 \times 0.6) = \$13.5$ commission after discount.

The difference is $22.5 - 13.5 = \$9$

15. Solution: 12.

16. Solution: 42.
The ratio of the number of animals can be obtained as follows:
$c : d = 2 : 9$ and $d : s = 3 : 7$ $\Rightarrow$ $c : d : s = 6 : 27 : 63 = 2 : 9 : 21$.

Then the ratio of the cost is then:
$(3 \times 2) : (2 \times 9) : (1 \times 21) = 2 : 6 : 7$.

So the cost for cats is calculated as follows:
$$\frac{2}{2+6+7} \times 945 = 126$$
The number of cats is $126 \div 3 = 42$.

Method 2:
$3c + 2d + s = 945$ \hfill (1)

$\dfrac{c}{d} = \dfrac{2}{9}$ $\Rightarrow$ $d = \dfrac{9c}{2}$ \hfill (2)

$\dfrac{d}{s} = \dfrac{3}{7}$ $\Rightarrow$ $s = \dfrac{7d}{3} = \dfrac{7}{3} \times \dfrac{9c}{2} = \dfrac{21c}{2}$ \hfill (3)

Substituting (2) and (3) into (1):
$3c + 2 \times \dfrac{9c}{2} + \dfrac{21c}{2} = 945$ $\Rightarrow$ $\dfrac{45c}{2} = 945$ $\Rightarrow$ $c = 42$.

17. Solution: 402.
$12 = 12 \times 1 = 6 \times 2 = 4 \times 3 = 3 \times 2 \times 2$.

We see that $3^5 = 243$ which is not a 2-digit number.
$2^5 \times 5^1 = 160$ which is not a 2-digit number.
$2^5 \times 3^1 = 96$
$2^3 \times 3^2 = 72$
$2^2 \times 3^3 = 108$ which is not a 2-digit number.
$2^1 \times 3^1 \times 5^2 = 150$ which is not a 2-digit number.
$2^2 \times 3^1 \times 5^1 = 60$
$2^1 \times 3^2 \times 5^1 = 90$
$2^2 \times 3^1 \times 7^1 = 84$
$2^2 \times 3^1 \times 11^1 = 132$ which is not a 2-digit number.

The answer is $96 + 72 + 60 + 90 + 84 = 402$.

Mathcounts Chapter Competition Practice   **Test 1**

18. Solution: (3, 1).
We only care about the side AC. Figure 1 shows that the side AC is translated five units to the right and figure 2 shows that the line segment $A'C'$ is translated two units downward. The coordinates of the midpoint of segment $A'C'$ are

$$x_M = \frac{x_1 + x_2}{2} = \frac{1+5}{2} = 3, \text{ and } y_M = \frac{y_1 + y_2}{2} = \frac{1+1}{2} = 1.$$

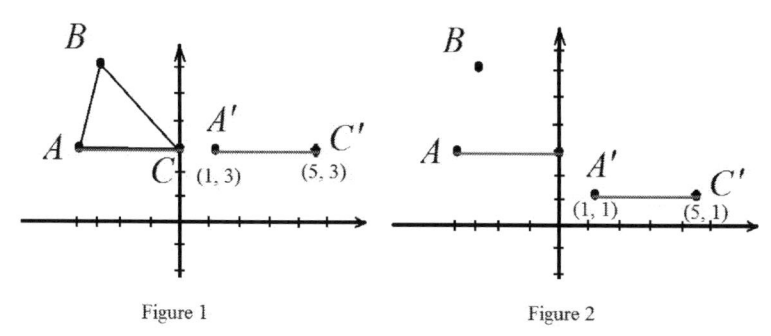

Figure 1

Figure 2

19. Solution: 11.
Let the integer be x.

$x^3 - x^2 = 1210$ ⇒ $x^2(x-1) = 11^2 \times 10 = 11^2 \times (11-1)$.
So $x = 11$.

20. Solution: D.

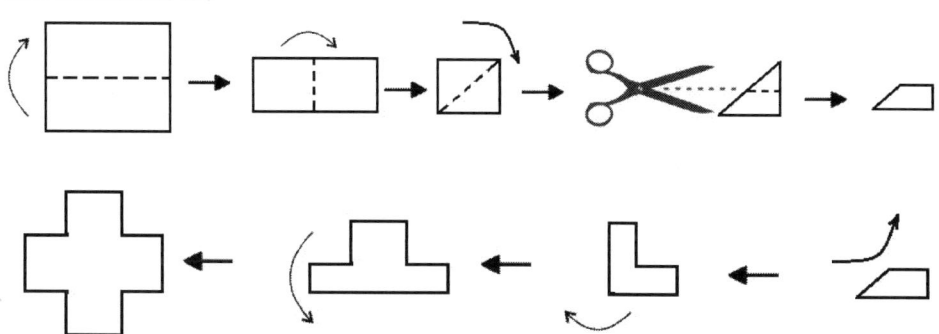

21. Solution: 37.
Since the average value of four numbers is 18, $a + b + c + d = 18 \times 4 = 72$ (1)

Mathcounts Chapter Competition Practice   **Test 1**

In order to get the greatest possible value of d, we let a be as small as possible.
So $a = 1$. Since $b - a = 7$, $b = 8$.
Substituting the values of a and b into (1): $c + d = 72 - 8 - 1 = 63$ (2)
We know that $d - c = 11$ (3)
(2) + (3): $2d = 74 \Rightarrow d = 37$.

22. Solution: 12.
A 4-digit positive integer is divisible by 15. So the last digit must be 0 and the sum of the digits must be divisible by 3.

The number can be 2490 or 2460. The units digit is fixed and other three digits can be exchanged.

We get 3! arrangements for 249 and 3! = 6 arrangements for 246. The answer is 6 + 6 = 12.

23. Solution: 180.
If the third number is 45, the second number could be either 75 or 15.

105 ← 75 ← 45
25 ← 75 ← 45
5   ← 15 ← 45
45 ← 15 ← 45.
The sum is 105 + 25 + 5 + 45 = 180.

24. Solution: 27.
Let the two-digit number be $10a + b$. The resulting umber be $10b + a$.
$\dfrac{10b+a}{4} + 9 = 10a + b \Rightarrow 10b + a + 36 = 40a + 4b \Rightarrow 6b + 36 = 39a \Rightarrow$
$2b + 12 = 13a \Rightarrow 2(b+6) = 13a$.
Since 2 and 13 are relatively prime, a must be a multiple of 2. Since a is a digit, it can be 2, 4, 6, or 8.
When a = 2, $2b + 12 = 13a \Rightarrow 2b + 12 = 13 \times 2 \Rightarrow 2b = 14 \Rightarrow b = 7$.

None of the values of 4, 6, 8 will work for a. So the answer is 27.

Mathcounts Chapter Competition Practice   Test 1

25. Solution: 12.
We will use the nth term formula $a_n = a_m + (n-m)d$ to solve this problem.
In figure 1, we label the numbers in the squares as a_1 and a_7. We know that $d_a = 40 - 45 = -5$. $a_n = a_m + (n-m)d$ $\Rightarrow$ $a_7 = a_1 + (7-1)d \Rightarrow$
$a_7 = 45 + (7-1)(-5) = 45 - 30 = 15$.

In figure 2, we label the numbers in the squares as b_1 and b_9. We know that $d_b = 15 - 18 = -3$. $a_n = a_m + (n-m)d$ $\Rightarrow$ $b_9 = b_1 + (9-1)(-3) = 18 - 24 = -6$.

In figure 3, we label the numbers in the squares as c_1 and c_8. We know that $d_c = -6 - (-9) = 3$. $a_n = a_m + (n-m)d$ $\Rightarrow$ $c_8 = c_1 + (8-1)(3) = -9 + 21 = 12$.

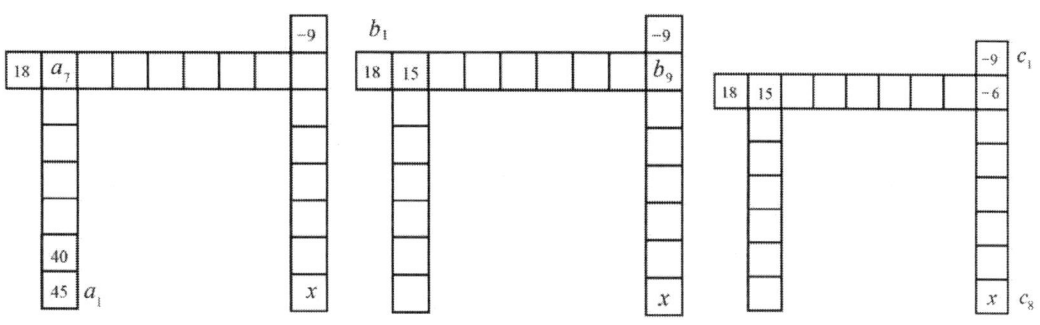

Figure 1   Figure 2   Figure 3

26. Solution: 12π.
Draw EF, the diameter from the tangent point. Let $EG = x$. We see that $GF = AB = 3\sqrt{3}$, and $AG = 6/2 = 3$.
$x \times 3\sqrt{3} = 3 \times 3 \Rightarrow$ $x = \sqrt{3}$.
So $EF = EG + GF = \sqrt{3} + 3\sqrt{3} = 4\sqrt{3}$.
So the radius is $\dfrac{4\sqrt{3}}{2} = 2\sqrt{3}$, and the area of the circle is 12π.

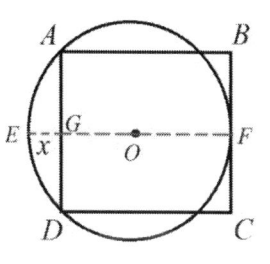

27. Solution: −64.
$f(n) = f(n-1) + 2f(n-2)$ (1)

Mathcounts Chapter Competition Practice   **Test 1**

$f(1) = 20$ and $f(3) = 16$
Let $n = 3$ in (1), we have $f(3) = f(2) + 2f(1)$ $\Rightarrow$ $f(2) = f(3) - 2f(1) = 16 - 2 \times 20 = -24$.
Let $n = 4$ in (1), we have $f(4) = f(3) + 2f(2) = 16 + 2 \times (-24) = -32$.
Let $n = 5$ in (1), we have $f(5) = f(4) + 2f(3) = -32 + 2 \times (16) = 0$.
Let $n = 6$ in (1), we have $f(6) = f(5) + 2f(4) = -0 + 2 \times (-32) = -64$.

28. Solution: 1.

$$x + \frac{1}{y} = y + \frac{1}{z} \Rightarrow x - y = \frac{1}{z} - \frac{1}{y} \Rightarrow x - y = \frac{y-z}{yz} \Rightarrow yz = \frac{y-z}{x-y} \quad (1)$$

$$x + \frac{1}{y} = z + \frac{1}{x} \Rightarrow x - z = \frac{1}{x} - \frac{1}{y} \Rightarrow x - z = \frac{y-z}{xy} \Rightarrow xy = \frac{y-z}{x-z} \quad (2)$$

$$y + \frac{1}{z} = z + \frac{1}{x} \Rightarrow y - z = \frac{1}{x} - \frac{1}{z} \Rightarrow y - z = \frac{z-x}{xz} \Rightarrow xz = \frac{z-x}{y-z} \quad (3)$$

(1) × (2) × (3): $(xyz)^2 = \frac{y-z}{x-y} \times \frac{x-y}{z-x} \times \frac{z-x}{y-z} = 1$.

Since we want to find the positive value of the product xyz, the answer is $xyz = 1$.

29. Solution: 19.
$1 + 2 + 3 + 4 + \ldots + 10 = 55$.
$55/4 = 13.75$.
So a, the side of the square, is less than or equal to 13.
Case 1: $a = 13$.
$10 + 3 = 9 + 4 = 8 + 5 = 7 + 6$ (1 square)

Case 2: $a = 12$.
$10 + 2 = 9 + 3 = 8 + 4 = 7 + 5$ (1 square)

Case 3: $a = 11$.
$10 + 1 = 9 + 2 = 8 + 3 = 7 + 4 = 6 + 5$ ($\binom{5}{4} = 5$ squares)

Case 4: $a = 10$.

Mathcounts Chapter Competition Practice   **Test 1**

$10 = 9 + 1 = 8 + 2 = 7 + 3 = 6 + 4$ ($\binom{5}{4} = 5$ squares)

Case 5: $a = 9$.

$9 = 8 + 1 = 7 + 2 = 6 + 3 = 5 + 4$ ($\binom{5}{4} = 5$ squares)

Case 6: $a = 8$.
$8 = 7 + 1 = 6 + 2 = 5 + 3$ (1 square)

Case 7: $a = 7$.
$7 = 6 + 1 = 5 + 2 = 4 + 3$ (1 square)

When $a \leq 6$, there is no square formed.

The answer is $1 + 1 + 5 \times 3 + 1 + 1 = 19$.

30. Solution: 7 cm^2.
Connect AF and BE. We know that the area of $\triangle AFG$ is the same as the area of $\triangle BEG = \sqrt{4 \times 9} = 6$ cm^2.

So the area of $\triangle ABF$ is $9 + 6 = 15$ cm^2, which is also the half of the area of the rectangle $ABCD$. So the area of the rectangle $ABCD$ is $2 \times 15 = 30$ cm^2.

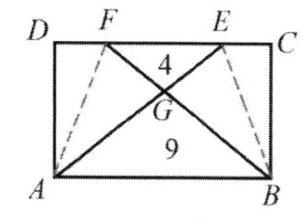

Thus the area of quadrilateral $BCEG$ is $30 - 10 - 9 - 4 = 7$ cm^2.

Mathcounts Chapter Competition Practice — Test 1

TARGET ROUND SOLUTIONS TO TEST 1

1. Solution: 7.

With a calculator, we easily compute: $\frac{1}{7} = 0.\overline{142857}$, $\frac{2}{7} = 0.\overline{285714}$, $\frac{3}{7} = 0.\overline{428571}$,

$\frac{4}{7} = 0.\overline{571428}$, $\frac{5}{7} = 0.\overline{714285}$, $\frac{6}{7} = 0.\overline{857142}$.

The pattern repeats every 6 digits (1, 2, 4, 5, 7, and 8 in some order).
$1 + 2 + 4 + 5 + 7 + 8 = 27$.

$2017 = 74 \times 27 + 19$.
Thus the sum of the first n digits ($n \leq 6$) must be 19.

We check all six expressions above and only get $4 + 2 + 8 + 5 = 19$ for $\frac{3}{7} = 0.\overline{428571}$,

and $5 + 7 + 1 + 4 + 2 = 19$ for $\frac{4}{7} = 0.\overline{571428}$.

So x can be 3 or 4. The sum is $3 + 4 = 7$.

2. Solution: 29.

Method 1:

The smallest possible value of d is $\left\lfloor \frac{50}{3} \right\rfloor + 1 = 17$.

Since $189 + 139 + 99 - 50 = 377$, d must be a factor of $377 = 29 \times 13$.
Since the smallest dividend is 99 and the sum of the remainders is 50, d must be less than 99.
Thus d must be 29.
When $d = 29$, $r_1 + r_2 + r_3 = 15 + 23 + 13 = 50$. So 29 works.
So the answer is 29.

Method 2:
$189 \equiv r_1 \pmod{d}$ (1)
$139 \equiv r_2 \pmod{d}$ (2)
$99 \equiv r_3 \pmod{d}$ (3)

Mathcounts Chapter Competition Practice Test 1

(1) + (2) + (3): $427 \equiv 50 \pmod{d}$ $\Rightarrow$ $377 \equiv 0 \pmod{d}$ (4)
d must be a factor of $377 = 29 \times 13$.

When $d = 13$, $r_1 + r_2 + r_3 = 7 + 9 + 8 = 24 < 50$.
When $d = 29$, $r_1 + r_2 + r_3 = 15 + 23 + 13 = 50$.
So the answer is 29.
Method 3:
$189 = a_1 d + r_1$ (1)
$139 = a_2 d + r_2$ (2)
$99 = a_3 d + r_3$ (3)

(1) + (2) + (3): $189 + 139 + 99 = d(a_1 + a_2 + a_3) + 50$ $\Rightarrow$

$$d(a_1 + a_2 + a_3) = 377 = 29 \times 13$$

d must be a factor of $377 = 29 \times 13$.
When $d = 13$, $r_1 + r_2 + r_3 = 7 + 9 + 8 = 24 < 50$.
When $d = 29$, $r_1 + r_2 + r_3 = 15 + 23 + 13 = 50$.
So the answer is 29.

3. Solution: 13.
Let C be the fruit (non-water) content of the oranges, V be the weight, and S be the substance.

	C	V	S
Before	0.1	5	0.5
After	0.2	x	$0.2x$

The substance does not change before or after the evaporating: $0.5 = 0.2x$ $\Rightarrow$ $x = 2.5$.
Alex actually paid $32.35/2.5 = \$12.94 \approx \$13$ per pound.

4. Solution: 2016.
Let the symbols $\bigcirc$, $\triangle$, $\diamondsuit$, and $\bigcirc\!\!\!\!\!\!\bigcirc$ represent numbers a, b, c, and d.

$a + b + c = 1007$ (1)
$a + b + d = 1008$ (2)
$a + c + d = 2015$ (3)
$b + c + d = 2018$ (4)

25

Mathcounts Chapter Competition Practice   **Test 1**

(1) + (2) + (3) + (4) : $3(a + b + c + d) = 6048$ (6)
(6) can be simplified into: $a + b + c + d = 2016$

5. Solution: 12.

Let six consecutive positive odd numbers be $2x + 1$, $2x + 3$, $2x + 5$, $2x + 7$, $2x + 9$, and $2x + 11$, where x is any non-negative integer.

The sum of them is $(2x + 1) + (2x + 3) + (2x + 5) + (2x + 7) + (2x + 9) + (2x + 11) = 12x + 36 = 12(x + 3)$.

The greatest whole number that must be a factor of $12(x + 3)$ is 12.

6. Solution: $13\sqrt{3}$.

The area of each hexagon is $6 \times \dfrac{\sqrt{3}}{4} a^2 = 6 \times \dfrac{\sqrt{3}}{4} \times 2^2 = 6\sqrt{3}$.

Each hexagon can be divided into six congruent triangle of area $\sqrt{3}$.
Note that the area of triangle ABE = the area of triangle CBD = the area of triangle AFC.
So the area of triangle ABC = the area of triangle DEF + 3 × the area of triangle ABE.
The area of triangle $DEF = 4 \times \sqrt{3}$.
The area of triangle ABE is the half of the area of parallelogram $AGBE$.
The area of parallelogram $AGBE$ is $6\sqrt{3}$.
The area of triangle ABE is $\dfrac{6\sqrt{3}}{2} = 3\sqrt{3}$.

The answer is $4\sqrt{3} + 3 \times 3\sqrt{3} = 13\sqrt{3}$.

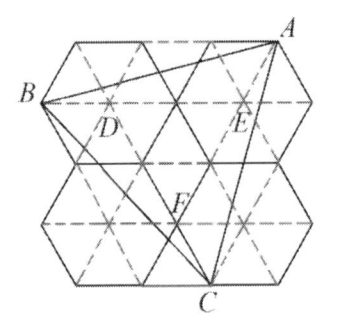

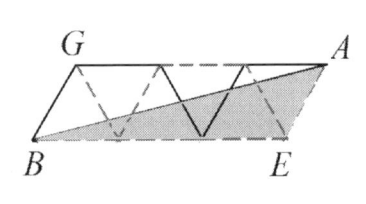

Mathcounts Chapter Competition Practice　　　　　　　　　　　**Test 1**

7. Solution: 16.

Since Charles paid $20, we can think that every needs to pay $20. So 5 loaves cost $60. Alex contributed 3 loaves, which cost $\frac{3}{5} \times 60 = 3 \times 12 = 36$. We know that he only needs to pay $20, so he needs to get back 36 – 20 = $16.

8. Solution: 6/15.
Chris says, "I know when Anna's birthday is"!
Chris must get either 5/17 or 6/15.
Bob says, "At first, I didn't know when Anna's birthday was". That means the month he got is not May.
Bob continues to say: "but I know now".
Since Bob knows the month, he knows that birthday only when the month he gets is 6.
So Anna's birthday is 6/15.

Mathcounts Chapter Competition Practice   **Test 2**

MATHCOUNTS

■ **Chapter Competition** ■
Practice Test 2
Sprint Round Problems 1–30

Name _____

DO NOT BEGIN UNTIL YOU ARE INSTRUCTED TO DO SO.

This round of the competition consists of 30 problems. You will have 40 minutes to complete the problems. You are not allowed to use calculators, books or any other aids during this round. If you are wearing a calculator wrist watch, please give it to your proctor now. Calculations may be done on scratch paper. All answers must be complete, legible and simplified to lowest terms. Record only final answers in the blanks in the right-hand column of the competition booklet. If you complete the problems before time is called, use the remaining time to check your answers.

Total Correct	Scorer's Initials

Mathcounts Chapter Competition Practice   **Test 2**

1. A gardener plans to build a fence to enclose a square garden plot. Seventeen fence posts are used to fence each side of the square plot. One post is placed at each corner. How many posts will he use to fence the entire plot?

2. A particular triangle has sides of length 15 cm, 12 cm and 9 cm. In square centimeters, what is the area of the triangle?

3. The difference of the squares of two positive integers is 17. What is the product of the two positive integers?

4. Kathy randomly picks up a clever integer defined as an even integer that is greater than 30, less than 200, and such that the sum of its digits is 9. What is the probability that the clever integer is divisible by 12? Express your answer as a common fraction.

5. Two graphs show the incomplete data from a small town about the percentages of people in four age groups (0 – 14 years old, 15 – 40 years old, 41 – 59 years old, and above 60 years old). How many people are in the age group from 41 to 59 years old?

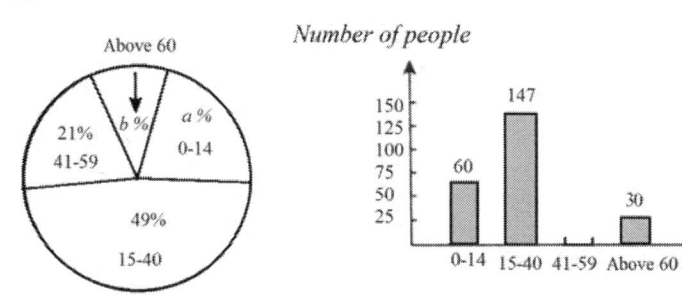

6. Solve for x: $\dfrac{1 - \dfrac{3x}{100}}{\dfrac{1}{10}} = \dfrac{1 - \dfrac{x}{20}}{\dfrac{1}{16}}$.

Mathcounts Chapter Competition Practice   **Test 2**

7. The points (x, y) represented in this table lie on a straight line. The point $(27, t)$ lies on the same line. What is the value of t?

x	y
1	9
3	17
5	25
27	t

8. In the sequence 2, 2, 4, 8, 2,..., each term after the second term is the units digit of the product of the previous two terms. What is the 2016th term?

9. A pizza costing $19.36 is cut into 8 equal pieces. Bill eats 3 pieces. In dollars, how much was the portion of the pizza that Bill ate? Express your answer as a decimal to the nearest hundredth.

10. Three squares are put on the table as shown. A_1, A_2, and A_3 are the areas of three squares. If $A_1 + A_2 = 2106$ cm^2, find A_3.

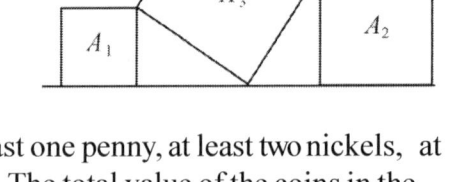

11. Richard has a piggy bank containing at least one penny, at least two nickels, at least three dimes, and at least four quarters. The total value of the coins in the piggy bank is $2.25. What is the sum of the largest possible number of nickels and the smallest possible number of nickels in the piggy bank?

12. On Friday, a snowboard originally priced at $100 was discounted 50%. On Monday, that sale price was reduced by 50%. On Tuesday, that sale price was reduced by 20%. On Wednesday, that sale price was reduced by 20%. In dollars, what is the price of the snowboard after the Wednesday reduction?

Mathcounts Chapter Competition Practice   **Test 2**

13. Let $a - 2b = 3c$ where a, b, and c are three consecutive terms in a positive geometric sequence. Find the value of a/b.

14. Calculate: $\dfrac{1}{1 \times 2 \times 3} + \dfrac{1}{2 \times 3 \times 4} + \dfrac{1}{3 \times 4 \times 5} + \dfrac{1}{4 \times 5 \times 6} + \dfrac{1}{5 \times 6 \times 7}$.

15. How many different letter arrangements can you get by picking up 4 letters from the word MATHCOUNTS?

16. An ant crawls along the edge of a regular hexagon from the vertex A clockwisely. How far is the ant from the vertex A after it craws 2016 inches? Each edge of the hexagon is 9 inches.

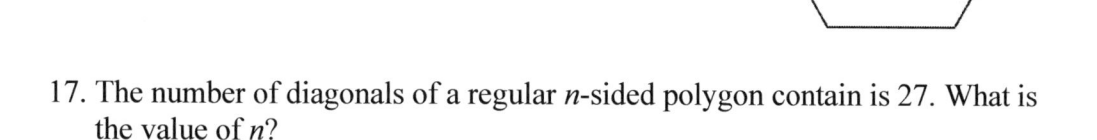

17. The number of diagonals of a regular n-sided polygon contain is 27. What is the value of n?

18. You are given five cards labeled 0, 2, 4, 6, and 9. How many different 4-digit numbers divisible by 12 can be formed using these cards? Note that rotation of cards is not allowed.

19. A unit fraction is a fraction with numerator 1. Some unit fractions can be written as the difference of two unit fractions with the positive integer denominators differing by 1. For example, $\dfrac{1}{6} = \dfrac{1}{2} - \dfrac{1}{3}$, $\dfrac{1}{20} = \dfrac{1}{4} - \dfrac{1}{5}$. How many unit fractions among all the unit fractions $\dfrac{1}{1}, \dfrac{1}{2}, \dfrac{1}{3}, \ldots, \dfrac{1}{200}$ cannot

be written as the difference of two unit fractions with the denominators differing by 1?

20. Assume you have 10 chips numbered 0, 1, 2, ..., 9 and that you choose 2 chips at random. What is the chance that at least one of these numbers is either 8 or 9? Express your answer as a common fraction.

21. If $|5x+2|<27$, find the sum of the distinct possible integer values of x.

22. The sum of the reciprocals of four consecutive positive integers is $\frac{19}{20}$. What is the sum of these four consecutive positive integers?

23. The accompanying graph describes the motion of a toy car across the floor for 8 seconds. What was the total distance in meters travelled by the toy car for the entire 8 second interval shown?

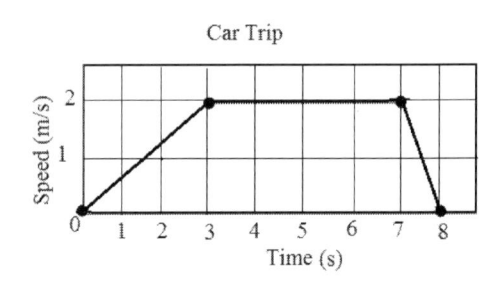

24. One hundred athletes are standing in a row facing Mr. Strong. Each athlete's jersey is numbered with one number from 1 to 100, consecutively.
Mr. Strong says: "If your number is a multiple of 4, please turn round". All athletes with the number on their jersey a multiple of 4 turn round.
Mr. Strong then says: "If your number is a multiple of 5, please turn round". All athletes with the number on their jersey a multiple of 5 turn round.
Mr. Strong last says: "If your number is a multiple of 6, please turn round". All athletes with the number on their jersey a multiple of 6 turn round.
How many athletes are facing Mr. Strong now?

Mathcounts Chapter Competition Practice   **Test 2**

25. Both a and b are real numbers with $2a^2 - 2ab + b^2 + 4a + 4 = 0$. Find the value of ab.

26. You are a traveler in city A and you must reach city B by nightfall or else you will be eaten by a lion. Obviously, you want to take the shortest path. How many ways can you go if you must follow the path from A to B?

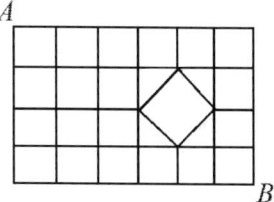

27. A regular pentagon and a regular hexagon are coplanar and share a common side AD, as shown. What is the degree measure of $\angle EAC - \angle BAC$?

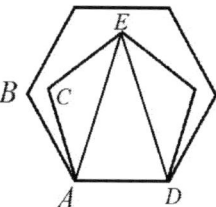

28. The coordinates of the vertices of a parallelogram are $(5, 8)$, $(3, -2)$, $(6, 1)$ and (x, y). What is the sum of the distinct possible values for x?

29. The first digit of a six-digit number $\overline{1abcde}$ is 1. The product of this six-digit number and 3 is $\overline{abcde1}$. Find $\overline{1abcde}$.

30. A particular right square-based pyramid has a volume of $\frac{5}{3}s$ cubic meters and a lateral height of $\frac{\sqrt{29}}{2}$ meters, where s is the side length of the square base. What is the greatest value of s?

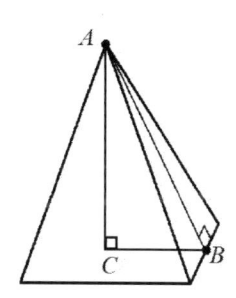

33

Mathcounts Chapter Competition Practice — Test 2

MATHCOUNTS

■ **Chapter Competition
Practice Test 2
Target Round Problems** ■

Name _____

DO NOT BEGIN UNTIL YOU ARE INSTRUCTED TO DO SO.

This round of the competition consists of eight problems, which will be presented in pairs. Work on one pair of problems will be completed and answers will be collected before the next pair is distributed. The time limit for each pair of problems is six minutes. The first pair of problems is on the other side of this sheet. When told to do so, turn the page over and begin working. Record your final answer in the designated space on the problem sheet. All answers must be complete, legible and simplified to lowest terms. This round assumes the use of calculators, and calculations may also be done on scratch paper, but no other aids are allowed.

Total Correct	Scorer's Initials

Mathcounts Chapter Competition Practice   **Test 2**

1. Each vertex of this parallelogram has integer coordinates. The perimeter of this parallelogram is p units, while the area is a square units. What is the value of the sum $p + a$? Express your answer in simplest radical form.

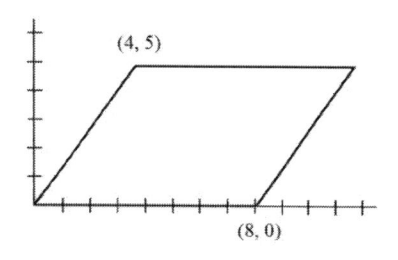

(4, 5)

(8, 0)

2. Mary adds all but two of the first 2016 positive integers. Her sum is a square number. What is the smallest possible number that Mary did not include?

Mathcounts Chapter Competition Practice   **Test 2**

3. What is the smallest positive integer that can be expressed as the sum of two different non-zero-perfect squares in two different ways?

4. Container A contains wine and water in the ratio of 3 : 1. Container B contains wine and water in the ratio of 1 : 5. You need to fill a third container C which holds seven gallons, in order that its contents may be half wine and half water. How many gallons of mixtures from container A should you use?

5. How many ways are there to select two small squares from the following 3 by 3 square grid such that two squares selected share the same vertex but not the same side?

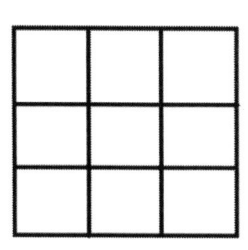

6. K is the set of natural numbers with the property that every element in K is not divisible by 3 and is not divisible by 4. But if a number is divisible by 3 or 4 and is also divisible by 5, the number is in K (like 15, 20, 60,…). Find the 79th smallest member of K.

Mathcounts Chapter Competition Practice   Test 2

7. *CF* is a diagonal of a regular hexagon *ABCDEF*. *P* is a point on *CF*. The area of the triangle *CBP* is 4 and the area of the triangle *EFP* is 5. What is the total number of square centimeters in the area of the regular hexagon *ABCDEF*?

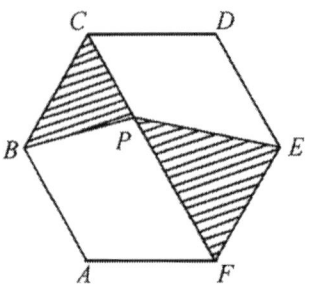

8. Anna whispers her birth month to Bob, and birth date to Chris. The boys don't know one another's numbers but they do know that the all possible birthdays are as follows:

5/12	5/13	5/17
6/14	6/15	
7/11	7/13	
8/11	8/12	8/14

   Chris says, "I don't know Anna's birthday".
   Bob says, "I don't know Anna's birthday either".
   Then Chris says, "Now I know Anna's birthday".
   Finally, Bob announces, "Now I also know Anna's birthday".
   When is Anna's birthday?

Mathcounts Chapter Competition Practice — Test 2

ANSWER KEYS TO TEST 2

SPRINT ROUND

1. 64.
2. 54.
3. 72.
4. 5/9.
5. 63.
6. 12.
7. 113.
8. 6.
9. $7.26.
10. 2016.
11. 20.
12. $16.
13. 3.
14. 5/21.
15. 3360.
16. $9\sqrt{3}$.
17. 9.
18. 26.
19. 187.
20. 17/45.
21. -5.
22. 18.
23. 12 meters.
24. 67.
25. 4.
26. 45.
27. 24°.
28. 14.
29. 142857.
30. 5.

TARGET ROUND

1. $56 + 2\sqrt{41}$.
2. 495.
3. 65.
4. 4.
5. 8.
6. 133.
7. 27.
8. 8/14.

Mathcounts Chapter Competition Practice — Test 2

SOLUTIONS TO TEST 2

SPRINT ROUND

1. Solution: 64.
If we do not count the corner posts, we have 15 posts in each side. $15 \times 4 = 60$.
Then we add the four posts at four corners. The answer is $60 + 4 = 64$.

2. Solution: 54.
The triangle is a 3-4-5 right triangle with two legs 9 and 12 cm. The area is $9 \times 12/2 = 54$ cm^2.

3. Solution: 72.
Let x and y be the two positive integers.
$$x^2 - y^2 = 17 \implies (x-y)(x+y) = 17.$$
Since both x and y be the two positive integers, and 17 is a prime number, we get $x = 9$ and $y = 8$. The product is $8 \times 9 = 72$.

4. Solution: 5/9.
We list all the clever integers: 36, 54, 72, 90, 108, 126, 144, 162, 180. There are 9 clever integers.

A positive integer that is divisible by 12 is divisible by 4. The last 2-digit must be divisible by 4.

We see that 36, 72, 108, 144, and 180 are divisible by 12.
The probability is 5/9.

5. Solution: 63.
Let x be the total number of people in this small town and y be the number of people in the age group of 41 to 59.
$$\frac{147}{49\%} = \frac{x}{100\%} \implies x = 300.$$
$y = 21\% \times 300 = 63$.

Mathcounts Chapter Competition Practice   Test 2

6. **Solution**: 12.

$$\frac{1-\frac{3x}{100}}{\frac{1}{10}} = \frac{1-\frac{x}{20}}{\frac{1}{16}} \quad\Rightarrow\quad 10(1-\frac{3x}{100}) = 16(1-\frac{x}{20})$$

$$\Rightarrow 10-\frac{3x}{10} = 16-\frac{4x}{5} \quad\Rightarrow\quad \frac{4x}{5}-\frac{3x}{10} = 16-10 \quad\Rightarrow\quad \frac{5x}{10} = 6 \quad\Rightarrow\quad \frac{x}{2} = 6 \quad\Rightarrow\quad x = 12.$$

7. **Solution**: 113.

Since the data show one straight line, we have $\frac{y_2-y_1}{x_2-x_1} = \frac{y_3-y_1}{x_3-x_1} \Rightarrow \frac{17-9}{3-1} = \frac{t-9}{27-1}$

$\Rightarrow \frac{8}{2} = \frac{t-9}{26} \Rightarrow t-9 = 4\times 26 \Rightarrow t = 113$.

8. **Solution**: 6.

The sequence is 2, 2, 4, 8, 2, 6, 2, 2, 4, 8, 2, 6,…. The pattern repeats every six terms: 2, 2, 4, 8, 2, 6.
2016 = 6 × 336. So the 2016th term is the same as the sixth term in the pattern, which is 6.

9. **Solution**: $ 7.26.

$\frac{3}{8}\times 19.36 = 7.26$.

10. **Solution**: 2016.

$\triangle ABC$ is congruent to $\triangle DEC$ ($\alpha = \alpha$, $\beta = \beta$, $c = c$).
$A_1 = a^2$, and $A_2 = b^2$.
By Pythagorean Theorem, $a^2 + b^2 = c^2$.
$A_1 + A_2 = A_3 = 2016$.

11. **Solution**: 20.

We have the equation: $p + 5n + 10d + 25q = 225 \quad\Rightarrow\quad 5n = 225 - p - 10d - 25q$

$\Rightarrow\quad n = 45 - 2d - 5q - \frac{p}{5}$.

41

We know the number of nickels is a positive integer. So the largest possible number of nickels in the piggy bank is $n = 45 - 2\times 3 - 5\times 4 - \dfrac{5}{5} = 18$.

The smallest possible number of nickels in the piggy bank is 2.
The answer is $18 + 2 = 20$.

12. **Solution:** $16.
The new sale price will be
$(1-50\%)(1-50\%)(1-20\%)(1-20\%) \times 100 = 0.5 \times 0.5 \times 0.8 \times 0.8 \times 100 = 16$.

13. **Solution:** 3.
Since a, b, and c are three consecutive terms in a geometric sequence, we have

$$b^2 = ac \text{ or } c = \dfrac{b^2}{a} \qquad (1)$$

Substituting (1) into the given equation $a - 2b = 3c$, we get $a - 2b = \dfrac{3b^2}{a} \Rightarrow$

$$a^2 - 2ab - 3b^2 = 0 \Rightarrow (\dfrac{a}{b})^2 - \dfrac{2a}{b} - 3 = 0 \qquad (2)$$

Let $\dfrac{a}{b} = x$. (2) becomes: $x^2 - 2x - 3 = 0 \qquad \Rightarrow (x+1)(x-3) = 0$.

Since a and b are positive, $\dfrac{a}{b} = x = 3$.

14. **Solution:** 5/21.

$\dfrac{1}{1\times 2\times 3} = \dfrac{1}{2}(\dfrac{1}{1\times 2} - \dfrac{1}{2\times 3})$, $\dfrac{1}{2\times 3\times 4} = \dfrac{1}{2}(\dfrac{1}{2\times 3} - \dfrac{1}{3\times 4})$, $\dfrac{1}{3\times 4\times 5} = \dfrac{1}{2}(\dfrac{1}{3\times 4} - \dfrac{1}{4\times 5})$,

$\dfrac{1}{4\times 5\times 6} = \dfrac{1}{2}(\dfrac{1}{4\times 5} - \dfrac{1}{5\times 6})$, $\dfrac{1}{5\times 6\times 7} = \dfrac{1}{2}(\dfrac{1}{5\times 6} - \dfrac{1}{6\times 7})$.

So $\dfrac{1}{1\times 2\times 3} + \dfrac{1}{2\times 3\times 4} + \dfrac{1}{3\times 4\times 5} + \dfrac{1}{4\times 5\times 6} + \dfrac{1}{5\times 6\times 7}$

$= \dfrac{1}{2}(\dfrac{1}{1\times 2} - \dfrac{1}{2\times 3} + \dfrac{1}{2\times 3} - \dfrac{1}{3\times 4} + \dfrac{1}{3\times 4} - \dfrac{1}{4\times 5} + \dfrac{1}{4\times 5} - \dfrac{1}{5\times 6} + \dfrac{1}{5\times 6} - \dfrac{1}{6\times 7})$

$= \dfrac{1}{2}(\dfrac{1}{1\times 2} - \dfrac{1}{6\times 7}) = \dfrac{1}{2}(\dfrac{21}{42} - \dfrac{1}{42}) = \dfrac{1}{2}(\dfrac{20}{42}) = \dfrac{10}{42} = \dfrac{5}{21}$.

Mathcounts Chapter Competition Practice — Test 2

15. Solution: 3360.
We divide the letters the following way:
(T, T),
(M, A, H. C, O, U, N, S).

Case 1: One "T" is used.
We have $\binom{9}{4} \times 4! = 3024$ arrangements.

Case 2: Two "T" are used.
We have $\binom{2}{2}\binom{8}{2} \times \dfrac{4!}{2!} = 336$ arrangements.

The answer is 3024 + 336 = 3360.

16. Solution: $9\sqrt{3}$.
2016 = 6 × 9 × 37 + 18 = 54 × 37 + 18.
The ant will be back the vertex A after 37 rounds. 18 = 9 + 9. So the ant is located at vertex B. Since the hexagon is regular, $\triangle ACD$ is a 30°− 60° − 90° right triangle. $AC = 9$ and $AD = \dfrac{9}{2}\sqrt{3}$.

The answer is $AB = 2AD = 2 \times \dfrac{9}{2}\sqrt{3} = 9\sqrt{3}$.

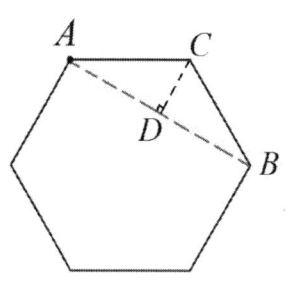

17. Solution: 9.
Method 1:
The number of diagonals is $\binom{n}{2} - n$, where n is the number of sides of a polygon.

We see that $\binom{9}{2} - 9 = 27$. So $n = 9$.

Method 2:

$\binom{n}{2} - n = 27 \Rightarrow \dfrac{n(n-1)}{2} - n = 27 \Rightarrow \dfrac{n^2 - n - 2n}{2} = 27$

$\Rightarrow n^2 - 3n - 54 = 0 \Rightarrow (n-9)(n+6) = 0$.

So n is 9.

18. **Solution:** 26.
The 4-digit numbers have the following properties:
(1) The number formed by the last two digits 2-digit must be divisible by 4,
We have 7 cases for the last two digits: 04, 20, 24, 40, 60, 64, 92, and 96.

(2) The sum of 4 digits must be divisible by 3.

We have
2604, 6204, 2904, 9204.
6420, 4620, 9420, 4920.
6924, 9624, 6024, 9024.
2940, 9240, 2640, 6240.
2460, 4260.
2064, 2964, 9264.
4092, 4692, 6492.
2496, 4296.

19. **Solution:** 187.
We see that $\dfrac{1}{2} = \dfrac{1}{1 \times 2}, \dfrac{1}{6} = \dfrac{1}{2} - \dfrac{1}{3}, \dfrac{1}{12} = \dfrac{1}{3} - \dfrac{1}{4}, \dfrac{1}{20} = \dfrac{1}{4} - \dfrac{1}{5}$.
So $1 \times 2, 2 \times 3, 3 \times 4, 4 \times 5, \ldots, 13 \times 14\ (=182), 14 \times 15\ (=210,$ which is over 200).

So we have 13 of them that are able to be written as the difference of two unit fractions with the denominators differing by 1. The answer is 200 – 13 = 187.

20. **Solution:** 17/45.
We use the indirect method to solve this problem.
Let us say, we just choose 2 chips from 8 chips numbered 0, 1, 2, 3, 4, 5, 6, and 7. We have no chance to choose chip 8 or 9.
The chance that at least one of these numbers is either 8 or 9 will be

$$1-\frac{\binom{8}{2}}{\binom{10}{2}} = 1 - \frac{28}{45} = \frac{17}{45}.$$

21. Solution: -5.
Case 1: $5x + 2 < 27$ $\Rightarrow$ $5x < 27 - 2 = 25$ $\Rightarrow$ $x < 5$
Case 2: $5x + 2 > -27$ $\Rightarrow$ $5x > -27 - 2 = -29$ $\Rightarrow$ $x > -5.8$
So x can be from -5 to 4.
We see that all the numbers from -4 to 4 will be canceled when we do the sum. So the answer is -5.

22. Solution: 18.
Let four numbers be x, $x + 1$, $x + 2$, and $x + 3$.
$$\frac{1}{x} + \frac{1}{x+1} + \frac{1}{x+2} + \frac{1}{x+3} = \frac{19}{20}$$
We know that $x < x + 1 < x + 2 < x + 3$, $\frac{1}{x} > \frac{1}{x+1} > \frac{1}{x+2} > \frac{1}{x+3}$.
So we have $\frac{1}{x} + \frac{1}{x} + \frac{1}{x} + \frac{1}{x} > \frac{19}{20} \Rightarrow \frac{4}{x} > \frac{19}{20} \Rightarrow \frac{1}{x} > \frac{19}{20} \times \frac{1}{4} \Rightarrow x < \frac{80}{19} = 4\frac{4}{19}$
We also have $\frac{1}{x+3} + \frac{1}{x+3} + \frac{1}{x+3} + \frac{1}{x+3} < \frac{19}{20} \Rightarrow \frac{4}{x+3} < \frac{19}{20} \Rightarrow x+3 > 4\frac{19}{20}$
$\Rightarrow x > 1\frac{19}{20}$.
Since x is an integer, x can be 2, 3, or 4.
Only when $x = 3$, we have $\frac{1}{3} + \frac{1}{3+1} + \frac{1}{3+2} + \frac{1}{3+3} = \frac{19}{20}$.
The answer is $3 + 4 + 5 + 6 = 18$.

23. Solution: 12 meters.
Method 1:
From 0 to 3 seconds, the average speed is 1 and distance travelled is $d = vt = 1 \times 3 = 3$ meters.
From 3 to 7 seconds, the average speed is 2 and distance travelled is $d = vt = 2 \times 4 = 8$ meters.

From 7 to 8 seconds, the average speed is 1 and distance travelled is $d = vt = 1 \times 1 = 1$ meters.
The total distance is $3 + 8 + 1 = 12$ meters

Method 2:
The total distance travelled by the toy car is the same as the area of the trapezoid:
$\frac{(4+8)2}{2} = 12$ meters.

24. **Solution:** 67.
Athletes with jersey number multiple of 4 only, multiple of 5 only, or multiple of 6 only, turn round one time and these athletes will not face Mr. Strong.

Athletes with jersey number multiple of 4 and 5, and 6 turn round three times and these athletes will not face Mr. Strong.

We use Venn diagram to solve the problem.
Step 1:
There is $\left\lfloor \frac{100}{lcm(4,5,6)} \right\rfloor = \left\lfloor \frac{100}{60} \right\rfloor = 1$ athlete whose jersey number is 60 (Figure 1).
Step 2:
There are $\left\lfloor \frac{100}{(4 \times 5)} \right\rfloor = \left\lfloor \frac{100}{20} \right\rfloor = 5$ athletes whose jersey number is a multiple of 20 (Figure 2).
There are $\left\lfloor \frac{100}{5 \times 6} \right\rfloor = \left\lfloor \frac{100}{30} \right\rfloor = 3$ athletes whose jersey number is a multiple of 30 (Figure 2).
There are $\left\lfloor \frac{100}{lcm(4 \times 6)} \right\rfloor = \left\lfloor \frac{100}{12} \right\rfloor = 8$ athletes whose jersey number is a multiple of 10 (Figure 2).
Step 3:
Athletes with jersey number multiple of 4 only: $\left\lfloor \frac{100}{4} \right\rfloor - 4 - 7 - 1 = 13$ (Figure 3).

Athletes with jersey number multiple of 5 only: $\left\lfloor \frac{100}{5} \right\rfloor - 4 - 2 - 1 = 13$ (Figure 3).

Mathcounts Chapter Competition Practice   **Test 2**

Athletes with jersey number multiple of 6 only: $\left\lfloor \dfrac{100}{6} \right\rfloor - 7 - 2 - 1 = 6$ (Figure 3).

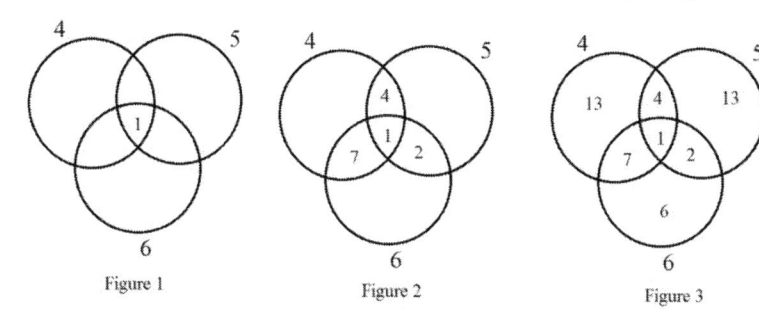

Figure 1   Figure 2   Figure 3

So the answer is $100 - 13 - 13 - 6 - 1 = 67$.

25. **Solution**: 4.

$2a^2 - 2ab + b^2 + 4a + 4 = 0 \Rightarrow a^2 - 2ab + b^2 + a^2 + 4a + 4 = 0 \Rightarrow$
$(a^2 - 2ab + b^2) + (a^2 + 4a + 4) = 0 \Rightarrow (a-b)^2 + (a+2)^2 = 0$.

Since a and b are real numbers, we have $(a+2)^2 = 0$ and $(a-b)^2 = 0$.
So we have $a = -2$ and $a = b = -2$. The answer is $(-2) \times (-2) = 4$.

26. **Solution**: 45.

We have two cases for the shortest paths (figures 1 and 2).

$A - C - D - B$: $\binom{5}{1} \times 1 \times \binom{3}{1} = 15$ ways.

$A - E - F - B$: $\binom{5}{2} \times 1 \times \binom{3}{1} = 30$ ways.

The answer is $15 + 30 = 45$ ways.

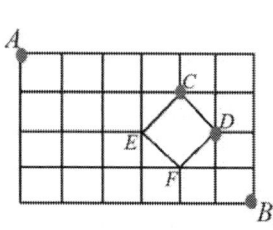

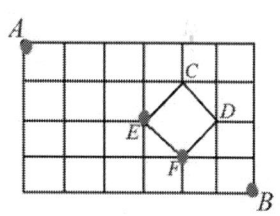

Figure 1   Figure 2

27. **Solution**: 24°.

$\angle DAB = \dfrac{180° \times (n-2)}{n} = \dfrac{180° \times (6-2)}{6} = 120°$.

$\angle DAC = \dfrac{180° \times (n-2)}{n} = \dfrac{180° \times (5-2)}{5} = 108°$.

$\angle BAC = \angle DAB - \angle DAC = 120° - 108° = 12°$.
$2\angle EAC = 180° - \angle ACE = 180° - \angle DAC = 180° - 108° = 72°$.
$\angle EAC = 36°$.
$\angle EAC - \angle BAC = 36° - 12° = 24°$.

28. **Solution:** 14.

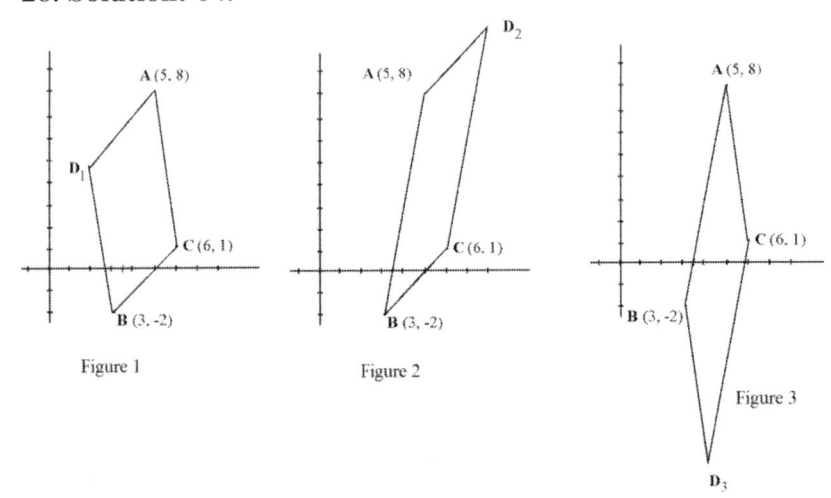

Figure 1

Figure 2

Figure 3

Given three vertices $A(x_A, y_A)$, $B(x_B, y_B)$, and $C(x_C, y_C)$, find the coordinates of the fourth vertex of a parallelogram:

$$x_D = x_A + x_C - x_B$$

For figure 1:
$x_{D_1} = 5 + 3 - 6 = 2$.

For figure 2:
$x_{D2} = 5 + 6 - 3 = 8$.

For figure 3:
$x_{D3} = 3 + 6 - 5 = 4$.

The answer is $2 + 8 + 4 = 14$.

29. **Solution:** 142857.

Let $\overline{abcde}$ be x.
$\overline{1abcde} = 100000 + \overline{abcde} = 100000 + x$.

48

$\overline{abcde1} = \overline{abcde0} + 1 = 10 \times \overline{abcde} + 1 = 10x + 1$.

We know that $3 \times (100000 + x) = 10x + 1$.

Solving we get $x = 42857$.
The answer is $\overline{1abcde} = 142857$.

30. **Solution:** 5.
Let the height be h.
By the volume formula, $\dfrac{5}{3}s = \dfrac{1}{3}s^2 h \Rightarrow sh = 5$ \qquad (1)

We know in right triangle ABC: $AB^2 = AC^2 + BC^2$ or

$(\dfrac{\sqrt{29}}{2})^2 = h^2 + (\dfrac{s}{2})^2 \Rightarrow 4h^2 + s^2 = 29$ \qquad (2)

(1) × 4: $4sh = 20$ \qquad (3)

(3) + (2): $4h^2 + s^2 + 4sh = 49 \Rightarrow (2h + s)^2 = 49$

$\Rightarrow 2h + s = 7 \Rightarrow 2h = 7 - s$ \qquad (4)

Substituting (4) into (1): $s(7 - s) = 10$

$\Rightarrow s^2 - 7s + 10 = 0 \Rightarrow (s - 5)(s - 2) = 0$

So $s = 5$ or 2 (ignored).

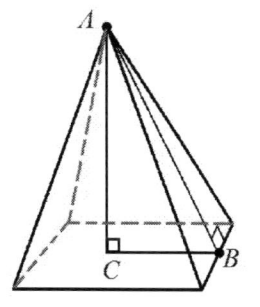

Mathcounts Chapter Competition Practice   Test 2

TARGET ROUND SOLUTIONS

1. Solution: $56 + 2\sqrt{41}$.

The base is 8 and the height is 5. The area is $8 \times 5 = 40$.

Using the distance formula, the length of the line segment connecting (0, 0) and (4, 5) is $\sqrt{(4-0)^2 + (5-0)^2} = \sqrt{41}$.
The perimeter if $2 \times 8 + 2 \times \sqrt{41}$.
The answer is $40 + 16 + 2\sqrt{41}$ or $56 + 2\sqrt{41}$.

2. Solution: 495.

The sum of the first 2016 positive integers is $\dfrac{(1+2016) \times 2016}{2} = 2033136$.

$\sqrt{2033136} \approx 1425.88$.
$1425^2 = 2030625$
The sum of the two numbers that she did not included is $2033136 - 2030625 = 2511$.
The smallest possible number she did not include is $2511 - 2016 = 495$.

3. Solution: 65.
We know that
$(a^2 + b^2)(c^2 + d^2) = (ac - bd)^2 + (bc + ad)^2$
$(a^2 + b^2)(c^2 + d^2) = (ac + bd)^2 + (bc - ad)^2$

We need to choose the smallest possible values for *a*, *b*, *c*, and *d* with $ac \neq bd$; $bc \neq ad$.
First we try $a = 1, b = 1, c = 2, d = 3$.
$(a^2 + b^2)(c^2 + d^2) = (1+1)(4+9) = 26$.
$26 = (2-3)^2 + (3+2)^2 = 1^2 + 5^2$
$26 = (2+3)^2 + (3-2)^2 = 5^2 + 1^2$.
We do not have two different non-zero-perfect squares.
We then try $a = 1, b = 2, c = 2, d = 2$.
$(a^2 + b^2)(c^2 + d^2) = (1+4)(4+4) = 40$.

50

$40 = (2-4)^2 + (4+2)^2 = 2^2 + 6^2$
$40 = (2+4)^2 + (4-2)^2 = 6^2 + 2^2$
We do not have two different non-zero-perfect squares.

Next we choose $a = 1, b = 2, c = 1, d = 3$.
$(a^2 + b^2)(c^2 + d^2) = (1+4)(1+9) = 50$.
$50 = (1-6)^2 + (2+3)^2 = 5^2 + 5^2$ (not the sum of two different non-zero-perfect squares).
$50 = (1+6)^2 + (2-3)^2 = 7^2 + 1^2$

Next we assign $a = 1, b = 2, c = 2, d = 3$.
$(a^2 + b^2)(c^2 + d^2) = (1+4)(4+9) = 65$.
$65 = (2-6)^2 + (4+3)^2 = 4^2 + 7^2$.
$65 = (2+6)^2 + (4-3)^2 = 8^2 + 1^2$.
So the smallest integer is 65.

4. **Solution:** 4.
We use the "C-V-S" method. C is the concentration or the strength of the solution. V is the volume of the solution. S is the substance of the solution.
Note: $C \times V = S$, $V_A + V_B = V_D$, and $S_A + S_B = S_D$. There is no relationship for C_A, C_B, and C_D.

Name	C	×	V	=	S
A	3/4	×	V_A	=	3/4 × V_A
			+		+
B	1/6	×	V_B	=	1/6 × V_B
			‖		‖
Mixture	1/2	×	7	=	7/2

$V_A + V_B = 7$ ⇒ $V_A = 1 - V_B$ (1)
$\frac{3}{4}V_A + \frac{1}{6}V_B = \frac{7}{2}$ (2)

Substituting (1) into (2): $V_B = 3$ and $V_A = 4$.

51

5. **Solution:** 8.

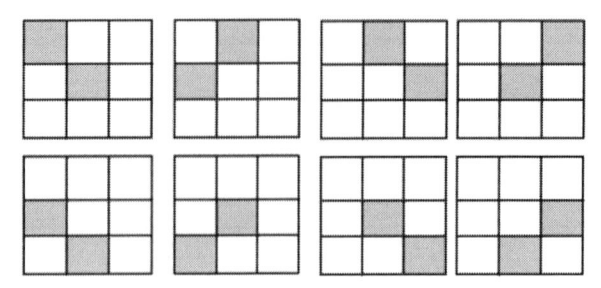

6. **Solution:** 133.
Method 1:
Let $a_{79} = n$.
$$79 = n - n(A \cup B) + n(A \cap C) + n(B \cap C) - n(A \cap B \cap C)$$
$$= n - \left\lfloor \frac{n}{3} \right\rfloor - \left\lfloor \frac{n}{4} \right\rfloor + \left\lfloor \frac{n}{3 \times 4} \right\rfloor + \left\lfloor \frac{n}{3 \times 5} \right\rfloor + \left\lfloor \frac{n}{4 \times 5} \right\rfloor - \left\lfloor \frac{n}{3 \times 4 \times 5} \right\rfloor \quad (1)$$

We know that $x - 1 < \lfloor x \rfloor \leq x$.

So $79 < n - (\frac{n}{3} - 1) - (\frac{n}{4} - 1) + \frac{n}{3 \times 4} + \frac{n}{3 \times 5} + \frac{n}{4 \times 5} - (\frac{n}{3 \times 4 \times 5} - 1) = \frac{3}{5}n + 3 \quad (2)$

and $79 > n - \frac{n}{3} - \frac{n}{4} + (\frac{n}{3 \times 4} - 1) + (\frac{n}{3 \times 5} - 1) + (\frac{n}{4 \times 5} - 1) - \frac{n}{3 \times 4 \times 5} = \frac{3}{5}n - 3 \quad (3)$

From (2) and (3) we get $126\frac{2}{3} < n < 136\frac{2}{3}$ or $127 \leq n \leq 136$.

We know that n is neither a multiple of 3 nor 4 (except a multiple of 5), so n must be one of 127, 130, 131, 133, 134, 135.
Substituting these possible values into (1), we see that the only solution is $n = 133$.

Method 2:
The least common multiple of 3, 4, and 5 is 60.
$$60 - \left\lfloor \frac{60}{3} \right\rfloor - \left\lfloor \frac{60}{4} \right\rfloor + \left\lfloor \frac{60}{3 \times 4} \right\rfloor + \left\lfloor \frac{60}{3 \times 5} \right\rfloor + \left\lfloor \frac{60}{4 \times 5} \right\rfloor - \left\lfloor \frac{60}{3 \times 4 \times 5} \right\rfloor = 36.$$

There are 36 terms in a_n from 1 to 60.
$a_1 = 1$, $a_2 = 2$, $a_3 = 5$, $a_4 = 7$, $a_5 = 10$, $a_6 = 11$ $a_7 = 13$, ..., $a_{36} = 60$.
We know that $79 = 36 \times 2 + 7$. So $a_{79} = 60 \times 2 + a_7 = 120 + 13 = 133$.

7. **Solution:** 27.

Mathcounts Chapter Competition Practice   Test 2

We divide the hexagon into six congruent smaller triangles. So the area of regular hexagon $S_{ABCDEF} = 6S_{\Delta OBC}$.

We connect BF and CE. $S_{BCEF} = 4S_{\Delta OBC}$.

$S_{\Delta CBP} + S_{\Delta EFP} = \dfrac{1}{2} S_{BCEF} = 2S_{\Delta OBC} = 2 \times \dfrac{S_{ABCDEFB}}{6} = \dfrac{S_{ABCDEFB}}{3} \Rightarrow$

$\dfrac{S_{ABCDEFB}}{3} = S_{\Delta CBP} + S_{\Delta EFP} \Rightarrow \dfrac{S_{ABCDEFB}}{3} = 4 + 5 = 9 \Rightarrow S_{ABCDEFB} = 27$.

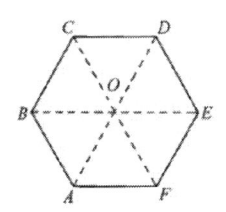

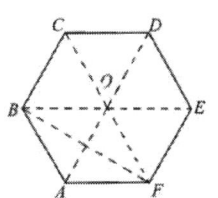

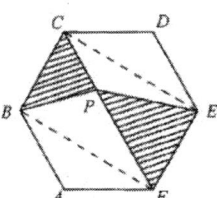

8. Solution: 8/14.
Chris knows the date. Since he is not sure about Anna's birthday, the date is neither 17 nor 15.
 The information left are:
  5/12   5/13   ~~5/17~~
  6/14   ~~6/15~~
  7/11   7/13
  8/11   8/12   8/14
Bob knows the month. Since he is not sure about Anna's birthday, the month is not 6. If the month were 6, he would know that the birthday were 6/14.

The information left are:
  5/12   5/13   ~~5/17~~
  ~~6/14~~   ~~6/15~~
  7/11   7/13
  8/11   8/12   8/14
Now Chris knows Anna's birthday. He must get 14. If the date were 11, 12, or 13, Chris would be not sure.
So Bob also knows that the date must be 14. Then both know Anna's birthday, which is 8/14.

Mathcounts Chapter Competition Practice — Test 3

MATHCOUNTS

■ **Chapter Competition** ■
Practice Test 3
Sprint Round Problems 1–30

Name _____

DO NOT BEGIN UNTIL YOU ARE INSTRUCTED TO DO SO.

This round of the competition consists of 30 problems. You will have 40 minutes to complete the problems. You are not allowed to use calculators, books or any other aids during this round. If you are wearing a calculator wrist watch, please give it to your proctor now. Calculations may be done on scratch paper. All answers must be complete, legible and simplified to lowest terms. Record only final answers in the blanks in the right-hand column of the competition booklet. If you complete the problems before time is called, use the remaining time to check your answers.

Total Correct	Scorer's Initials

Mathcounts Chapter Competition Practice   Test 3

1. Betsy has collected $6.25 in nickels and dimes. She has exactly 41 dimes. How many nickels does she have?

2. One of the following four-digit numbers is not divisible by 4: 20184, 20174, 20164, 20144, 20104. What is the product of the units digit and the tens digit of that number?

3. The heights for Alex, Bob, Cathy, Debra, and Emma are 147 cm, 149 cm, 150 cm, 151 cm, and 153 cm, respectively. Find Frank's height that is 3 cm less than the average height of five students mentioned before.

4. What is the greatest three-digit number which is a multiple of 17?

5. Each small square in the diagram of 3 by n grid below is colored red (R), yellow (Y) or blue (B). What is the least value of n to guarantee that at least two columns are colored exactly the same way?

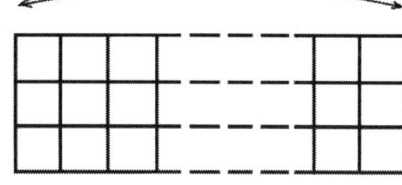

6. The numbers 1 through 110 are written on 110 cards with one number on each card. Sally picks one of the 110 cards at random. What is the probability that the number on her card will be a multiple of 5 or 11? Express your answer as a common fraction.

7. Alex is a publisher who published a book a year ago. He paid the author $20,000. The cost for printing a copy of the book was $15. He also paid the bookstore 30% of the sale price of $30 each book. He managed to get 10% profit at the end of the year. Find the least number of copies of the book sold.

Mathcounts Chapter Competition Practice   Test 3

8. Bob received five email messages yesterday in the following order: A, B, C, D, and E. Whenever he opened his mail box, he always replied the most recent message first. Which one of the following is the possible order he replied to the five messages:

   (1) ABECD   (2) BAECD   (3) CEDBA   (4) DCABE   (5) ECBAD

9. Using each of the digits only once, in how many ways can the digits 1, 3, 5, and 7 be placed, one digit per box, such that 0. ☐☐ > 0. ☐☐.

10. The line $y = 2016 + 504x$ contains points in how many quadrants of the Cartesian coordinate plane?

11. The time is 9:00. The hour hand is pointing west on a 12-hour clock. Which direction (north, south, east or west) is the hour hand pointing 75 hours later?

12. Six equilateral triangles each with side length 1 can form a regular hexagon of the side length 1. How many such equilateral triangles are required to form a regular hexagon of side length 6?

13. Determine the ratio of the surface area of a rectangular prism to its volume if its length, width, and height are the zeroes of the polynomial $x^3 - 3x^2 + 13x - 15 = 0$. Express your answer as a common fraction.

14. Let 7, 11, and c be the lengths of the sides of a triangle. If c is an integer, then what is the difference between the largest and smallest possible value of c?

Mathcounts Chapter Competition Practice   **Test 3**

15. A taxi driver charges the rates as follows:
    First person: $4 for first mile, $0.40 for each additional 1/3 mile.
    Additional people: $3.3 for each additional person.
    If five people share a 32.5-mile ride, how many dollars is the total cost of the ride?

16. How many square units are in the area of the convex quadrilateral with vertices (0, 0), (0, 5), (3, 4), and (7, 0)? Express your answer as a mixed number.

17. Alex and Bob run a lap in 100 seconds and 150 seconds respectively around a 900 m track in opposite directions and starting from the same point. How many meters does Bob need to continue to run to reach the starting point when they meet for the ninth time (not counting the start)?

18. In how many ways can 36 be written as the sum of two primes?

19. Sam uses exactly 100 non-overlapping square tiles, each 1 cm by 1cm, to make four squares. How many ways are there to do so?

20. If we let $(2\sqrt{2} + \sqrt{7})^{2016} = m$, find the expression of $(2\sqrt{2} - \sqrt{7})^{2016}$ in terms of m.

21. There exist positive integers x, y, and z satisfying $29x + 30y + 31z = 366$. Compute the value of $x + y + z$.

22. Gauss Math Club bought some math books for the winners of their school math competitions last year. Table below shows the number of copies of each book they purchased and the total cost.

Mathcounts Chapter Competition Practice   **Test 3**

| Purchase date | \multicolumn{5}{c}{Books} | Total cost |

Purchase date	A	B	C	D	E	Total cost
Dec. 15, 2014	1	3	4	5	6	$2,016
Mar. 20, 2014	1	5	7	9	11	$3,499

What is the cost to buy one book of each kind?

23. A printer is used to print out the squares of the first 30 positive integers. How many digits are printed by the printer?

24. If the volume of a regular tetrahedron is tripled without changing its height, by what factor is the length of each side increased? Express your answer in simplest radical form.

25. Sally has a bag which at the start contains 15 red marbles and 20 white marbles. When she draws out a red marble, she puts the marble back and adds four more red marbles. When she draws out a white marble, she puts the marble back and adds seven more white marbles. What is the fewest number of rounds of draws/replacements/additions after which the bag could contain exactly 75 marbles?

26. What is the sum of all two-digit positive integers that can be written with the digits 1, 2, 3 and 4 if no digit is allowed to use more than one time in each two-digit positive integer?

27. If x and y are positive integers each less than 20 for which $2(x-y)^3 + 4y^2 = 254$, what is the sum of all possible positive integer value for x?

28. When its digits are reversed, a particular positive three-digit integer is increased by 20%. What is the original number?

Mathcounts Chapter Competition Practice Test 3

29. Two congruent regular hexagons *ABCDEF* and *PQRSTV* are placed such that *P* is on the center of the hexagon *ABCDEF* as shown. If the area of each hexagon is 6, find the area of the shaded region.

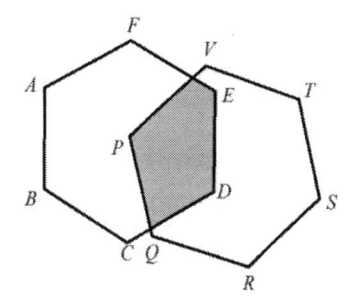

30. Each day, four out of the six teams in a class are randomly selected to participate in a MATHCOUNTS trial competition. What is the probability that Team *A* is selected at least two of the next four days? Express your answer as a common fraction.

MATHCOUNTS

■ **Chapter Competition
Practice Test 3
Target Round Problems** ■

Name _____

DO NOT BEGIN UNTIL YOU ARE INSTRUCTED TO DO SO.

This round of the competition consists of eight problems, which will be presented in pairs. Work on one pair of problems will be completed and answers will be collected before the next pair is distributed. The time limit for each pair of problems is six minutes. The first pair of problems is on the other side of this sheet. When told to do so, turn the page over and begin working. Record your final answer in the designated space on the problem sheet. All answers must be complete, legible and simplified to lowest terms. This round assumes the use of calculators, and calculations may also be done on scratch paper, but no other aids are allowed.

Total Correct	Scorer's Initials

Mathcounts Chapter Competition Practice   Test 3

1. A container has 25 balls each colored green or blue. Alex takes out one half of the green balls and one third of the blue balls. Find the least number of balls Alex takes out.

2. If Emily rolls a standard six-sided die five times, what is the probability that she rolls two different values in the first two rolls and the same value in the last three rolls? Express your answer as a common fraction.

Mathcounts Chapter Competition Practice   Test 3

3. *AB* and *CD* are two chords of the circle O intersecting at point P. $\angle APD = 60°$. If the length of arc *AD* is 3π and the length of arc *BC* is 5π, find the circle's area. Express your answer in terms of π.

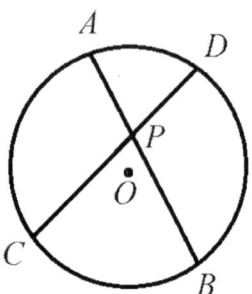

4. In the figure shown, a circle passes through two adjacent vertices of a rectangle *ABCD* (with $AB = 3\sqrt{3}$, and $AD = 6$) and is tangent to the opposite side of the rectangle. What is the shaded area? Express your answer in terms of π.

Mathcounts Chapter Competition Practice   Test 3

5. In the arithmetic sequence a_n, $a_2 + a_5 + a_8 = 9$, and $a_2 \times a_5 \times a_8 = 15$. Find the product of all the possible values of d, the common difference. Express your answer as a common fraction.

6. Find the sum of the greatest and the smallest possible values of $|x-5|+|x-7|$ if $0 \leq x \leq 8$.

7. How many line segments can be counted in the figure? Note that a dot is an endpoint of segment.

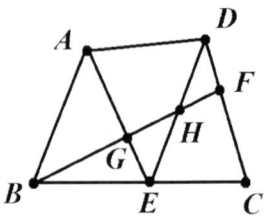

8. Three distinct numbers are selected simultaneously and at random from the set {1, 2, 3, 4, 5, 6, 7, 8, 9, 10}. What is the probability that their product is an even number? Express your answer as a common fraction.

Mathcounts Chapter Competition Practice — Test 3

ANSWER KEYS TO TEST 3

SPRINT ROUND

1. 43.
2. 28.
3. 147 cm.
4. 986.
5. 28.
6. $\dfrac{3}{11}$
7. 4889.
8. (3).
9. 12.
10. 3.
11. North.
12. 216.
13. $\dfrac{26}{15}$.
14. 12.
15. $55.
16. $21\dfrac{1}{2}$.
17. 360.
18. 4.
19. 5.
20. $n = 1/m$.
21. 12.
23. 78.
24. $\sqrt{3}$.
25. 7.
26. 330.
27. 13.
28. 495.
29. 2.
30. 8/9.

TARGET ROUND

1. 9.
2. $\dfrac{5}{216}$.
3. 144π.
4. $9\sqrt{3} - 4\pi$.
5. $-\dfrac{4}{9}$.
6. 14.
7. 20.
8. $\dfrac{11}{12}$.

SOLUTIONS TO TEST 3

SPRINT ROUND

1. **Solution:** 43.
$625 - 41 \times 10 = 215$
$215/5 = 43$.

2. **Solution:** 28.
A number is divisible by 4 if the last two-digit of the number is divisible 4. So the number that is not divisible by 4 is 20174. The answer is $7 \times 4 = 28$.

3. **Solution:** 147 cm.
The average of the heights of Alex, Bob, Cathy, Debra, and Emma is $(147 + 149 + 150 + 151 + 153)/5 = 5 \times 150/5 = 150$.
So Frank's height is $150 - 3 = 147$ cm.

4. **Solution:** 986.
$1000 \div 17 = 58$ R 14
Since the remainder is 14,
$1000 - 14 = 986$.

5. **Solution:** 28.
Each column has three small squares. Each square has three ways to color. So each column there are $3 \times 3 \times 3 = 27$ ways to color. By the pigeonhole principle, we need at least $27 + 1 = 28$ columns to guarantee that at least two columns are colored exactly the same way.

6. **Solution:** $\dfrac{3}{11}$
Let n be the number of terms from 1 to 110 that is a multiple of 5 or 11.
$$n = \left\lfloor \frac{110}{5} \right\rfloor + \left\lfloor \frac{110}{11} \right\rfloor - \left\lfloor \frac{110}{5 \times 11} \right\rfloor = 22 + 10 - 2 = 30.$$
The probability is $P = \dfrac{30}{110} = \dfrac{3}{11}$.

Mathcounts Chapter Competition Practice   **Test 3**

7. **Solution:** 4889.
Let x be the number of the copies sold.

$1.1 (20{,}000 + 15x) = 30x - 0.3 \times 30 \times x \quad \Rightarrow \quad x = 4888.89 \approx 4889.$

8. **Solution:** (3).

In the answers (1) and (2), D should be after E. In (4), A should be after B. In (5), we do not see D after E.

The answer is (3).

9. **Solution:** 12.

Method 1:
We list:
$0.75 > 0.31$, $0.75 > 0.13$, $0.73 > 0.51$, $0.73 > 0.15$, $0.71 > 0.53$, $0.71 > 0.35$
$0.57 > 0.31$, $0.57 > 0.13$, $0.53 > 0.17$, $0.51 > 0.37$
$0.37 > 0.15$, $0.35 > 0.17$.
The answer is $6 + 4 + 2 = 12$.

Method 2:
If the tenths digit of the first decimal is 7, no matter how we place the rest of the 3 digits, the inequality will be true. So we have $3! = 6$ ways for this case.
If the tenths digit of the first decimal is 5, we have two ways (3, or 1, but not 7) to select the tenth digit of the second decimal in order for the inequality to be true. Then we have two digits left and we have two ways to order them. So we have $2 \times 2 = 4$ ways for this case.

If the tenths digit of the first decimal is 3, we have one way (1 only) to place the tenth digit of the second decimal in order for the inequality to be true. Then we have two digits left and we have two ways to order them. So we have $1 \times 2 = 2$ ways for this case.

The answer is $6 + 4 + 2 = 12$.

10. Solution: 3.
The line $y = 2016 + 504x$ is plotted using two points (0, 2016), (-4, 0) as follows:
As can be seen the line goes through 3 quadrants.

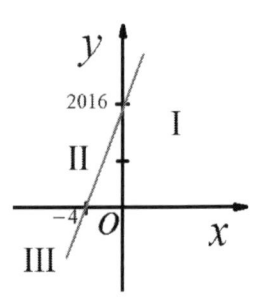

11. Solution: north.
$75/12 = \dfrac{75}{12} = \dfrac{25}{4} = 6\dfrac{1}{4}$.

The hour hand goes through $6\dfrac{1}{4}$ revolutions. If the hour hand started facing west, it'll end up facing north.

12. Solution: 216.

The ratio of the areas A to B as shown in the figure is $\dfrac{S_A}{S_B} = \left(\dfrac{6}{1}\right)^2$.

So we need 36 equilateral triangles each with side length 1 to make the larger equilateral triangles each with side length 6. To make a regular hexagon of side length 6, we need six equilateral triangles each with side length 6. So the answer is $36 \times 6 = 216$.

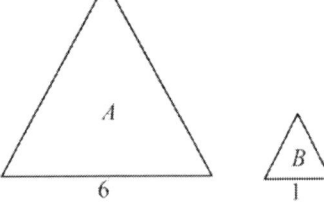

13. Solution: $\dfrac{26}{15}$.

If r, s, t are roots, by Vieta's Theorem,
$rs + st + tr = 13$
$rst = -(-15) = 15$.
The surface area is $2(rs + st + tr)$ and the volume is rst.
The ratio is $\dfrac{2(st + rt + rs)}{rst} = \dfrac{2 \times 13}{15} = \dfrac{26}{15}$.

14. Solution: 12.
By triangle inequality theorem, $11 - 7 < c < 11 + 7$ $\Rightarrow$ $4 < c < 18$.
Since c is an integer, the largest and smallest possible value of c are 17 and 5.

The answer is 17 – 5 = 12.

15. **Solution:** $55.
32.5 – 1 = 31.5.
31.5 ÷ (1/3) = 94.5
94.5 × 0.4 = 37.8
Thus the charge for the first person is: 4 + 37.8 = 41.8
The other people are $3.2 each regardless of the length of the trip. 41.8 + (3.3 × 4)
= 41.8 + 13.2 = $55.

16. **Solution:** $21\frac{1}{2}$.

Method 1:
The quadrilateral looks as follows:
The quadrilateral can be broken into a rectangle with width 3 units and length 4 units, 2 right triangles ($\triangle ABE$ and $\triangle BCD$).
The area is $3 \times 4 + \frac{1 \times 3}{2} + \frac{4 \times 4}{2} = 12 + \frac{3}{2} + 8 = 21\frac{1}{2}$.

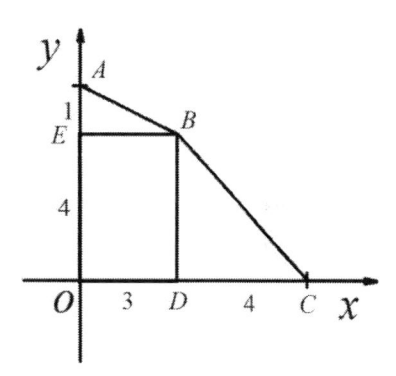

Method 2:

By the shoelace formula, the area is $A = \frac{1}{2} \begin{vmatrix} 0 & 0 \\ 0 & 5 \\ 3 & 4 \\ 7 & 0 \\ 0 & 0 \end{vmatrix}$

$= \frac{1}{2} \times |0 + 0 + 0 + 0 - (0 + 28 + 15 + 0)| = \frac{1}{2} \times |-43| = \frac{43}{2} = 21\frac{1}{2}$.

17. **Solution:** 360.
Alex's speed is 900/100 = 9 m/s. Bob's speed is 900/150 = 6 m/s.
Let t be the time taken for them to meet in every lap: $t(9 + 6) = 900 \Rightarrow t = 60$ seconds.
When they meet for the ninth time, Bob runs 9 × 60 = 540 seconds and 540 × 6 = 3240 meters.

$3240 = 900 \times 3 + 540$.
So Bob runs 3 laps and 540 meters already. He needs to run $900 - 540 = 360$ meters to reach the starting point.

18. Solution: 4.
We have the following prime numbers: 2, 3, 5, 7, 11, 13, 17, 19, 23, 29, 31.
$36 = 31 + 5 = 29 + 7 = 23 + 13 = 19 + 17$.
The answer is 4 ways.

19. Solution: 5.
The problem is the same as the following one:
How many ways are there to write 100 as the sum of four square numbers?

To determine what these squares could be, list all squares under 100:
1, 4, 9, 16, 25, 36, 49, 64, 81.

If 81 is chosen then three other numbers must sum to 19. We only see that $9 + 9 + 1 = 19$.

If 64 is chosen, three other numbers must sum to 36. We only see that $16 + 16 + 4 = 36$.

If 49 is chosen, three other numbers must sum to 51. We see that $49 + 1 + 1 = 25 + 25 + 1 = 51$.

If 25 is chosen, three other numbers must sum to 75. We only see that $25 + 25 + 25 = 75$.
Total we have 5 ways.

20. Solution: $n = 1/m$.
Let $(2\sqrt{2} - \sqrt{7})^{2016} = n$ \hfill (1)

We are given that $(2\sqrt{2} + \sqrt{7})^{2016} = m$ \hfill (2)

(1) × (2): $(2\sqrt{2} - \sqrt{7})^{2016} (2\sqrt{2} + \sqrt{7})^{2016} = m \times n \Rightarrow$

Mathcounts Chapter Competition Practice   **Test 3**

$(\sqrt{8}-\sqrt{7})^{2016}(\sqrt{8}+\sqrt{7})^{2016} = m \times n \Rightarrow ((\sqrt{8}-\sqrt{7})(\sqrt{8}+\sqrt{7}))^{2016} = m \times n \Rightarrow$
$(8-7)^{2016} = m \times n \Rightarrow m \times n = 1 \Rightarrow n = 1/m.$

21. **Solution:** 12.
Method 1:
We notice something special about the numbers 29, 30, 31, and 366. It is a leap year with 29 days in February, 30 days in April, June, September, November, and 31 days in January, March, May, July, August, October, and December.
So $x = 1$, $y = 4$, and $z = 7$. $x + y + z = 12$ (months).

Method 2:
$29x + 30y + 31z = 366$
$29(x + y + z) + y + 2z > 29(x + y + z) \Rightarrow$ $366 > 29(x + y + z) \Rightarrow (x + y + z) < 12.62$ (1)
$31(x + y + z) - 2x - y < 31(x + y + z) \Rightarrow$ $366 < 31(x + y + z) \Rightarrow (x + y + z) > 11.8$ (2)
From (1) and 2), we get $11.8 < x + y + z < 12.6$.
Since x, y, and z are positive integers, $x + y + z = 12$.

22. **Solution:** 533.
Let a, b, c, d, and e be the unit price for A, B, C, D, and E, respectively.
$a + 3b + 4c + 5d + 6e = 2016$ (1)
$a + 5b + 7c + 9d + 11e = 3499$ (2)
(1) × 2: $2a + 6b + 8c + 10d + 12e = 4032$ (3)
(3) – (2): $a + b + c + d + e = 533$.
Note: $a = 106$, $b = 108$, $c = 109$, $d = 110$, and $e = 100$ will work,

Or (2) – (1): $2b + 3c + 4d + 5e = 1483$ (4)
    (1) – (4): $a + b + c + d + e = 533$.

23. **Solution:** 78.
The first 3 squares are single digits (1, 4, 9). The next 6 squares are double digits (16, 25, 36, 49, 64, 81). The rest of 21 squares must be triple digits (100, 121, 144, 169, 196, 225, ..., 900).
$3 \times 1 + 6 \times 2 + 21 \times 3 = 3 + 12 + 63 = 78.$

Mathcounts Chapter Competition Practice   **Test 3**

24. Solution: $\sqrt{3}$.

Let V_1 be the volume of the new tetrahedron and V_2 be the volume of the original tetrahedron. a is the length of each side. h is the height.

$$V_1 = \frac{1}{3} \times \frac{\sqrt{3}}{4} a_1^2 h_1 \qquad (1)$$

$$V_2 = \frac{1}{3} \times \frac{\sqrt{3}}{4} a_2^2 h_2 \qquad (2)$$

$(1) \div (2)$: $\dfrac{V_1}{V_2} = \dfrac{\frac{1}{3} \times \frac{\sqrt{3}}{4} \times a_1^2 h_1}{\frac{1}{3} \times \frac{\sqrt{3}}{4} \times a_2^2 h_2} = (\dfrac{a_1}{a_2})^2 = 3 \quad \Rightarrow \quad \dfrac{a_1}{a_2} = \sqrt{3}$.

25. Solution: 7.

When Sally draws out a red marble, the number of red marbles will be increased by 4.
When Sally draws out a white marble, the number of white marbles will be increased by 7.

Since we want the fewest number of rounds of draws/replacements/additions, we consider more 7's possible.
We see clearly that:
R   15   4   4   4
W   20   7   7   7   7

$15 + 20 + 4 \times 3 + 7 \times 4 = 75$. The answer is $3 + 4 = 7$.

26. Solution: 330.

Method 1:
The two-digit numbers are: 12, 13, 14, 21, 23, 24, 31, 32, 34, 41, 42, 43. The sum is 330.

Method 2:
We have 4 ways to select the units digit and 3 ways to select the tens digit. So we have $4 \times 3 = 12$ such 2-digit numbers. We have $12 \times 2 = 24$ digits together. $24/4 =$

6. Each digit is used 6 times in these 12 numbers. Each digit is used 6/2 = 3 times in units digit position as well as the tens digit position. So we have
$3 \times (1+2+3+4) \times 11 = 330$.

27. **Solution:** 13.
$2(x-y)^3 + 4y^2 = 254$ $\Rightarrow$ $(x-y)^3 + 2y^2 = 127$ $\Rightarrow$ $(x-y)^3 = 127 - 2y^2$
Since 127 is odd and $2y^2$ is even, $(x-y)^3$ must be odd. We know that x and y are positive integers, so if we let $y = 1$, we get $(x-y)^3 = 127 - 2 = 125 = 5^3$.
So $x = 6$. We can also let $y = 8$, we get $(x-y)^3 = 127 - 128 = -1 = (-1)^3$. So $x = 7$.
The sum is $6 + 7 = 13$.

28. **Solution:** 495.
$\frac{120}{100}(100a + 10b + c) = 100c + 10b + a$ $\Rightarrow$ $6(100a + 10b + c) = 5(100c + 10b + a)$
$\Rightarrow 600a + 60b + 6c = 500c + 50b + 5a$ $\Rightarrow$ $595a + 10b = 494c$ $\Rightarrow$
$5(119a + 2b) = 494c$

Since 5 and 494 is relatively prime, c must be a multiple of 5. We know that c is a digit. So c can only be 5.

Then we have $119a + 2b = 494$

Since both $2b$ and 494 are even, $119a$ must be even. So the digit a must be even and it can be 2, 4, 6, or 8. Only $a = 4$ works. When $a = 4$, $b = 9$.

The original number is 495. We see that $1.2 \times 495 = 594$.

29. **Solution:** 2.

Draw $PN \perp EF$, $PM \perp CD$ (Figure 1).

We slide the hexagons $PQRSTV$ such that PN is overlapped with PV (Figure 2). The shaded area is $\frac{4}{12} \times 6 = 2$.

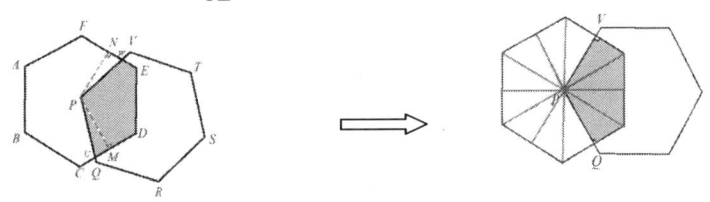

Figure 1   Figure 2

Mathcounts Chapter Competition Practice   **Test 3**

30. **Solution:** 8/9.

Method 1:
Let us say the names of the six teams are *A, B, C, D, E,* and *F*.

The number of ways to select 4 teams out of 6 teams is $\binom{6}{4} = \binom{6}{2} = 15$.

The number of ways Team *A* being selected is: $\binom{1}{1}\binom{5}{3} = 10$.

So Team *A* has a 10/15 = 2/3 probability of competing on any given day. We have three cases where team *A* competes:

(C: compete; N: Not compete).

Day 1   Day 2   Day 3   Day 4
C   N   N   C $P_1 = \frac{2}{3} \times \frac{1}{3} \times \frac{1}{3} \times \frac{2}{3} \times \frac{4!}{2! \times 2!} = \frac{24}{81}$

Day 1   Day 2   Day 3   Day 4
C   N   C   C $P_2 = \frac{2}{3} \times \frac{1}{3} \times \frac{2}{3} \times \frac{2}{3} \times \frac{4!}{3!} = \frac{32}{81}$

Day 1   Day 2   Day 3   Day 4
C   C   C   C $P_3 = \frac{2}{3} \times \frac{2}{3} \times \frac{2}{3} \times \frac{2}{3} = \frac{16}{81}$

The answer is $P_1 + P_2 + P_3 = \frac{24}{81} + \frac{32}{81} + \frac{16}{81} = \frac{8}{9}$.

Method 2 (indirect way):
Let us say the names of the seven teams are *A, B, C, D, E,* and *F*.

The number of ways to select 4 teams out of 6 teams is $\binom{6}{4} = \binom{6}{2} = 15$.

The number of ways team *A* being selected is: $\binom{1}{1}\binom{5}{3} = 10$.

So team *A* has a 10/15 = 2/3 probability of competing on any given day.

Mathcounts Chapter Competition Practice   **Test 3**

We have two cases where team A is not selected more than two day of the next four days
(C: compete; N: Not compete).

Day 1	Day 2	Day 3	Day 4
N	N	N	N

$$P_1 = \frac{1}{3} \times \frac{1}{3} \times \frac{1}{3} \times \frac{1}{3} = \frac{1}{81}$$

Day 1	Day 2	Day 3	Day 4
C	N	N	N

$$P_2 = \frac{2}{3} \times \frac{1}{3} \times \frac{1}{3} \times \frac{1}{3} \times \frac{4!}{3!} = \frac{8}{81}$$

The answer is $1 - (P_1 + P_2) = 1 - (\frac{1}{81} + \frac{8}{81}) = \frac{72}{81} = \frac{8}{9}$.

Mathcounts Chapter Competition Practice   **Test 3**

TARGET ROUND SOLUTIONS

1. **Solution:** 9.
Let g be the number of green balls and b be the number of blue balls. y be the number of balls Alex takes out.
$b + g = 25$
$$y = \frac{b}{2} + \frac{g}{3} = \frac{b}{2} + \frac{25-b}{3} = \frac{b}{2} + \frac{25}{3} - \frac{b}{3} = \frac{b+50}{6}.$$
Since we want the least value of y, we let $b = 4$ to get $y = 9$.

2. **Solution:** $\dfrac{5}{216}$.

Method 1:
We have two cases:
Emily rolls $ABCCC$, $ABAAA$, or $ABBBB$, where each letter represents a different digit.
In the first case, the probability is $P_1 = 1 \times \dfrac{5}{6} \times \dfrac{4}{6} \times \dfrac{1}{6} \times \dfrac{1}{6} = \dfrac{20}{6^4}$

In the second case, the probability is $P_2 = 1 \times \dfrac{5}{6} \times \dfrac{1}{6} \times \dfrac{1}{6} \times \dfrac{1}{6} = \dfrac{5}{6^4}$.

In the third case, the probability is $P_3 = 1 \times \dfrac{5}{6} \times \dfrac{1}{6} \times \dfrac{1}{6} \times \dfrac{1}{6} = \dfrac{5}{6^4}$.

The probability is $P = P_1 + P_2 = \dfrac{20}{6^4} + \dfrac{5}{6^4} + \dfrac{5}{6^4} = \dfrac{5}{216}$.

Method 2:
$P = 1 \times \dfrac{5}{6} \times 1 \times \dfrac{1}{6} \times \dfrac{1}{6} = \dfrac{5}{216}$.

3. **Solution:** 144π.
$\angle APD = \dfrac{\widehat{AD} + \widehat{BC}}{2} = \dfrac{3\pi + 5\pi}{2} = 4\pi$.
$\angle APC = 120° = 2\angle APD \quad \Rightarrow \quad \angle APC = \dfrac{\widehat{AC} + \widehat{DB}}{2} = 8\pi$
$\Rightarrow \quad \widehat{AC} + \widehat{DB} = 16\pi$.

Mathcounts Chapter Competition Practice   **Test 3**

So the circumference of the circle is $16\pi + 8\pi = 24\pi$ and the radius is $2\pi r = 24\pi \Rightarrow r = 12$.
The area of the circle is $\pi \times 12^2 = 144\pi$.

4. **Solution:** $9\sqrt{3} - 4\pi$.

Draw EF, the diameter from the tangent point. Let $EG = x$. We see that $GF = AB = 3\sqrt{3}$, and $AG = 6/2 = 3$.

$x \times 3\sqrt{3} = 3 \times 3 \Rightarrow \quad x = \sqrt{3}$.

So $EF = EG + GF = \sqrt{3} + 3\sqrt{3} = 4\sqrt{3}$.

So the radius is $\dfrac{4\sqrt{3}}{2} = 2\sqrt{3}$, and the area of the circle is 12π.

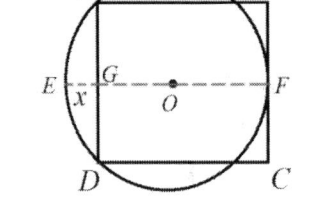

Connect OM, ON, and MN. $MP = 3$, $OM = 2\sqrt{3}$, so $OP = \sqrt{3}$, and $PF = \sqrt{3}$.

Since $OM = 2OP$, right triangle MOP is a 30°-60°-90° right triangle. So $\angle MON = 120°$.

The area of sector $MON = \dfrac{1}{3} \times 12\pi = 4\pi$.

The area of sector $MPN = 4\pi - 3\sqrt{3}$.

The shaded area is then the area of rectangle $BCNM$ – the area of sector $MPN = 6 \times \sqrt{3} - (4\pi - 3\sqrt{3}) = 9\sqrt{3} - 4\pi$.

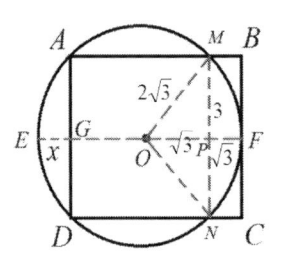

5. **Solution:** $-\dfrac{4}{9}$.

Method 1:
We observe $a_5 = 3$, $a_2 = 1$, and $a_8 = 5$.

     By the formula, $a_5 = a_2 + (5-2)d \quad \Rightarrow \quad 3 = 1 + (5-2)d \quad \Rightarrow \quad d = \dfrac{2}{3}$

We also know that the following terms are also work: $a_5 = 3$, $a_2 = 5$, and $a_8 = 1$.

     By the formula, $a_5 = a_2 + (5-2)d \quad \Rightarrow \quad 3 = 5 + (5-2)d \Rightarrow \quad d = -\dfrac{2}{3}$

So the answer is $\frac{2}{3} \times (-\frac{2}{3}) = -\frac{4}{9}$.

Method 2:

We know that $a_2 = a_5 - 3d$, and $a_8 = a_5 + 3d$.

So $a_2 + a_5 + a_8 = 9 \Rightarrow a_5 - 3d + a_5 + a_5 + 3d = 9 \Rightarrow a_5 = 3$.

$a_2 \times a_5 \times a_8 = 15 \Rightarrow (a_5 - 3d) \times a_5 \times (a_5 + 3d) = 15 \Rightarrow a_5 \times [a_5^2 - (3d)^2] = 15$

$\Rightarrow 9 - 9d^2 = 5 \Rightarrow 9d^2 = 4 \Rightarrow d^2 = \frac{4}{9} \Rightarrow d = \pm\frac{2}{3}$

So the answer is $\frac{2}{3} \times (-\frac{2}{3}) = -\frac{4}{9}$.

6. **Solution:** 14.

Method 1:

We get rid of the absolute value signs by examining three regions:

(1) $0 \le x \le 5$:
$|x-5| + |x-7| = 5 - x + 7 - x = 12 - 2x$.
The greatest value is 12 when $x = 0$.

(2) $5 < x \le 7$:
$|x-5| + |x-7| = x - 5 + 7 - x = 2$.

(3) $7 < x \le 8$: $|x-5| + |7-x|$.
The greatest value is 4 when $x = 8$
So the answer is $12 + 2 = 14$.

Method 2:
$|x-5| + |x-7|$ is the sum of the distances from x to 5 and to 8. The greatest distance is $5 + 7 = 12$ obtained when $x = 0$. The smallest distance is $1 + 1 = 2$ obtained when $5 \le x \le 7$. So the answer is 14.

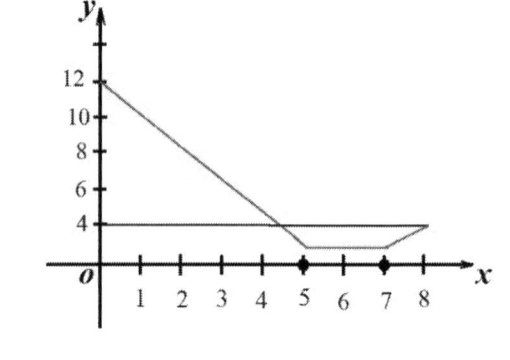

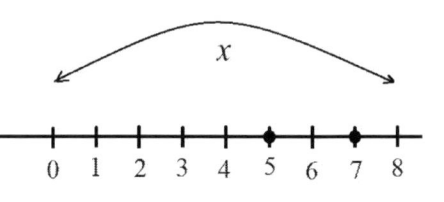

Method 3: We know that $|a| + |b| \ge |a + b|$. $|x-5| + |x-7| = |x-5| + |7-x|$ $\ge |x - 5 + 7 - x| = 2$. The smallest value is 2. We also know that the greatest value of $|x-5| + |x-7|$ is 12 when $x = 0$. So the answer is $12 + 2 = 14$.

Mathcounts Chapter Competition Practice   Test 3

7. **Solution:** 20.
Method 1:
AB, AG, AE, AD.
BG, BH, BF, BE, BC.
CD, CF, CE.
DE, DH, DF.
EG, EH.
We get $4 + 5 + 3 + 3 + 2 + 2 + 1 = 20$.
Method 2:

We get at most $\binom{8}{2} = 28$ line segment from eight points.

But we are not able to count AF, AH, AC, BD, EF, CH, CG, and DG. $28 - 8 = 20$.

8. **Solution:** $\dfrac{11}{12}$.

There are $\binom{10}{3} = 120$ possible ways to select three numbers.

We divide ten numbers into two groups:
(1, 3, 5, 7, 9) and (2, 4, 6, 8, 10)
Only when at least one value is even can we get an even product.

We have three cases:
Case 1: Even × Even × Even.

We have the following ways to select three even numbers: $\binom{5}{3} = 10$

Case 2: Even × Even × Odd.

We have the following ways to select one even and two odd numbers: $\binom{5}{2}\binom{5}{1} = 50$

Case 3: Even × Odd × Odd.

We have the following ways to select one even and two odd numbers: $\binom{5}{1}\binom{5}{2} = 50$

The answer is $P = \dfrac{10 + 50 + 50}{120} = \dfrac{11}{12}$.

MATHCOUNTS

■ **Chapter Competition** ■
Practice Test 4
Sprint Round Problems 1–30

Name _____

DO NOT BEGIN UNTIL YOU ARE INSTRUCTED TO DO SO.

This round of the competition consists of 30 problems. You will have 40 minutes to complete the problems. You are not allowed to use calculators, books or any other aids during this round. If you are wearing a calculator wrist watch, please give it to your proctor now. Calculations may be done on scratch paper. All answers must be complete, legible and simplified to lowest terms. Record only final answers in the blanks in the right-hand column of the competition booklet. If you complete the problems before time is called, use the remaining time to check your answers.

Total Correct	Scorer's Initials

Mathcounts Chapter Competition Practice   Test 4

1. Todd had 2016 baseball cards. He sold 1/3 of them and then gave away 3/7 of his remaining ones. How many cards does Todd have left?

2. Bob has a bag of marbles. Among them, 35% are green, 20% are yellow, and 80% of the remaining ones are blue. Find the number of marbles in the bag if the number of blue marbles is 36.

3. If 74 hens eat 47 kilograms of wheat and lay 888 eggs in 74 days, what is the average number of eggs produced per hen?

4. Ten containers labeled 1 through 10 in order are placed in a row. The number of marbles in any one container except container 1 is two times the number of marbles in the container before it. If container 9 has 512 marbles and container 10 has 1024 marbles, what is the number of marbles in container 5?

5. The formula $d = 11t^2$ is used to calculate the distance, d, in meter, a free falling object, starting from rest, will travel in t seconds. How many kilometers will the object travel in 11 seconds? Express your answer as a decimal to the nearest thousandth.

6. What is the sum of the reciprocals of the positive integer factors of 24? Express your answer as a common fraction.

7. Point P is on AB. Point A has coordinates (4, 12) and point B has coordinates (20, 6). The ratio of $AP : PB = 2 : 3$. Find the sum of the coordinates of point P.

8. What is the smallest integer whose cube is greater than 30,000?

9. Apples are distributed to 100 kids such that every kid gets at least one apple and each kid gets a different number of apples. Find the least number of apples needed.

10. Chelsea had a bag of balls with half of them red and half of them white. She added 15 red and 3 white balls to the bag. The fractional part of red balls is 3/5. How many balls are in the bag after addition?

11. Define $m \# n = mn - m - n + 11$ for all positive integers m and n. Find the value of $x + y$ if $x \# y = 21$.

12. What is the difference between the sum of all positive integers from 1 to 100 and the sum of all square numbers from 1 to 100?

13. The sum of a number, x, and its reciprocal is 6. What is the smallest value of x? Express your answer in simplest radical form.

14. A container has 25 balls green or blue. Alex takes out one half of the green balls and one third of blue balls. Find the greatest number of balls Alex takes out.

15. Triangle ABC is an equilateral triangle with side length of 6. The triangle is turned without sliding along a straight line 756 times as shown in the figure. Find the distance travelled by point A. Express your answer in terms of π.

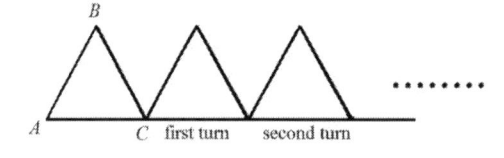

16. Find the probability that a randomly selected positive integer less than or equal to 2016 is divisible by 21? Express your answer as a common fraction.

17. A developer has 100 acres and he would like to divide it into smaller lots. Some should be 30 acres, some should be 15 acres, and some should be 5 acres. If the developer must have at least one lot of each type, how many different ways can he divide up the 100 acres?

Mathcounts Chapter Competition Practice   **Test 4**

18. Find the perimeter of a right triangle whose hypotenuse is 2 and whose area is 1. Express your answer in simplest radical form.

19. A bag of food is enough to feed 16 ducks and 12 chickens for 6 days. The same bag of food can feed 9 ducks and 10 chickens for 8 days. If this bag of food is used to feed only 8 chickens, how many days will it last? Assume that each duck eats at a constant rate every day and each chicken also eats at a different constant rate every day.

20. Three squares of side lengths 7 cm, 8 cm, and 5 cm are put together to form a new figure as shown. Points A, B, and C are vertices of the squares. Line segment CE divides the figure into two parts of the same area. What is the number of centimeter in the length of AE?

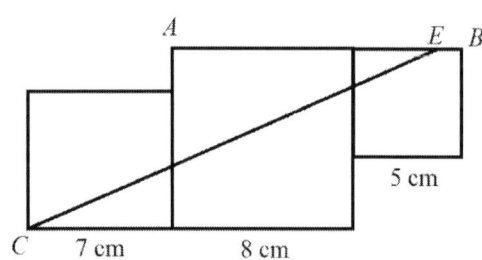

21. A jar contains 7 red, 11 blue and 13 yellow marbles. Blue marbles are then added in order to change the probability of randomly selecting a blue marble from the jar to "greater than 2/3." What is the least number of blue marbles that must be added?

22. The circumference of circle A is 12π and the circumference of circle B is 4π. Circle B rolls around the inside of circle A without slipping. When P first returns to its original position, what is the number of revolutions it must make?

83

Mathcounts Chapter Competition Practice   **Test 4**

23. A white cylindrical silo has a diameter of 8/π feet and a height of 21 feet. A wire is painted on the silo, as shown, making three and half revolutions around it. What is the length of the wire in feet? Express your answer in simplest radical form.

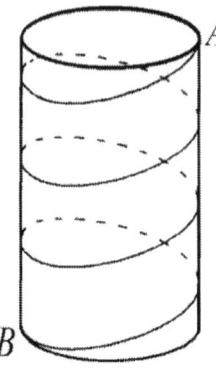

24. What is the probability that a randomly selected three-digit whole number is divisible by 3 and the hundreds digit is also 3? Express your answer as a common fraction.

25. Alex rides half of the time at the rate of 9 miles per hour and the rest of the time at the rate of 6 miles per hour for a journey of 90 miles. It takes him x hours to ride the first 45 miles and y hours to ride the second 45 miles. Find the value of $y - x$.

26. How many continuous paths starting from E, along the segments of the figure, and back to E, do not revisit any of the segments?

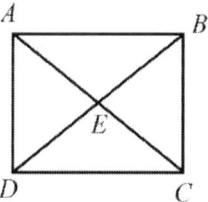

27. Find B if $\dfrac{B}{1221} = 0.3\overline{A7}$, where B is a positive integer and A is a digit in the repeating decimal representation.

Mathcounts Chapter Competition Practice   **Test 4**

28. The minute hand of a clock measures 7 cm from its tip to the center of the clock face, and the hour hand from its tip to the center of the clock face is 4 cm. What is the positive difference of the distances, in centimeters, traveled by the tips of both hands in 72 hours? Express your answer in terms of π.

29. The addition problem below has a unique solution. Each of the letters represents a different digit. Find the sum of all possible values of three-digit number *DEF* if *DEF* is also a prim number.

$$ABC$$
$$+ DEF$$
$$\overline{DGBD}$$

30. The sum of 3 positive real numbers is 12 and the sum of their squares is 54. What is the largest possible value for one of the numbers?

85

Mathcounts Chapter Competition Practice — Test 4

MATHCOUNTS

■ **Chapter Competition** ■
Practice Test 4
Target Round Problems

Name _____

DO NOT BEGIN UNTIL YOU ARE INSTRUCTED TO DO SO.

This round of the competition consists of eight problems, which will be presented in pairs. Work on one pair of problems will be completed and answers will be collected before the next pair is distributed. The time limit for each pair of problems is six minutes. The first pair of problems is on the other side of this sheet. When told to do so, turn the page over and begin working. Record your final answer in the designated space on the problem sheet. All answers must be complete, legible and simplified to lowest terms. This round assumes the use of calculators, and calculations may also be done on scratch paper, but no other aids are allowed.

Total Correct	Scorer's Initials

Mathcounts Chapter Competition Practice **Test 4**

1. Square *ABCD* of side length 8 cm shares the same vertex *D* with the rectangle *DEFG* of length 10 cm as shown. *E* is on *AB* and *C* is on *FG*. What is the number of square centimeters in the area of the rectangle *DEFG*?

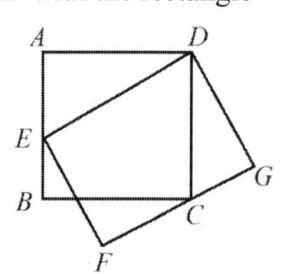

2. A utility company needs to install 20 electricity poles along a new road 1000 meters away. The space between each pole is 50 meters. The truck can carry at most three poles each time. Find the number of kilometers the truck travels in the job.

3. A large cube is constructed from individual unit cubes and then dipped into paint. Thereafter, it is disassembled into the original unit cubes; 492 of these have exactly two face painted. What is the side length of the large cube?

4. A large rectangle is divided into eight smaller rectangles. The area of each region is shown in the figure. What is the value of $x^2 + y^2 + z^2$?

x	y	z	16
81	x	y	z

Mathcounts Chapter Competition Practice   Test 4

5. The Fibonacci Sequence is the series of numbers: 1, 1, 2, 3, 5, 8, 13, 21, 34, ... The next number is found by adding up the two numbers before it. How many terms in the first 2016 terms in the sequence have the remainder 2 when divided by 3?

6. How many of the natural numbers from 1 to 700, inclusive, contain the digit 4 at least once? (The numbers 142 and 443 are two natural numbers that contain the digit 4 at least once, but 136 is not.)

Mathcounts Chapter Competition Practice   **Test 4**

7. An 5 × 5 grid of squares with two shaded squares is given. How many different rectangles bounded by the gridlines do not contain the shaded square?

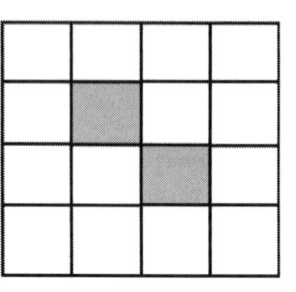

8. You are given 2016 squares. The side lengths of these squares are $1, \frac{1}{2}, \frac{1}{3}, \frac{1}{4}, \ldots, \frac{1}{2015}$, and $\frac{1}{2016}$. You need to fit all of them into a large square without overlapping. What is the smallest possible value for the side length of the large square? Express your answer as a common fraction.

Mathcounts Chapter Competition Practice — Test 4

ANSWER KEYS TO TEST 4

SPRINT ROUND

1. 768.
2. 100.
3. 12.
4. 32.
5. 1.331 km.
6. 5/2.
7. 20.
8. 32.
9. 5050.
10. 60.
11. 14.
12. 4,665.
13. $3 - 2\sqrt{2}$.
14. 12.
15. 2016π.
16. 1/21.
17. 6.
18. $2 + 2\sqrt{2}$.
19. 13 days.
20. 12 cm.
21. 30.
22. 2.
23. $30 + \sqrt{73}$.
24. $\dfrac{17}{450}$.
25. 2 hours.
26. 24.
27. 473.
28. 960π.
29. 396.
30. 6.

TARGET ROUND

1. 64.
2. 21 km.
3. 43.
4. 4788.
5. 756.
6. 214.
7. 44.
8. $\dfrac{3}{2}$.

Mathcounts Chapter Competition Practice   Test 4

SPRINT ROUND SOLUTIONS

1. **Solution:** 768.
Todd sold 1/3 of 2016 bards. The number of cards left is
$$2016 - \frac{1}{3} \times 2016 = 2016 \times \frac{2}{3} = 1344.$$

Todd sold 3/7 of 1344 bards. The number of cards left is
$$1344 - \frac{3}{7} \times 1344 = 1344 \times \frac{4}{7} = 768.$$

2. **Solution:** 100.
Method 1:
The fractional part of the number of marbles that are neither green nor yellow is
$$1 - \frac{35}{100} - \frac{20}{100} = \frac{45}{100}.$$

Since 80% of the remaining ones are blue, the fractional part of the number of blue is
$$\frac{80}{100} \times \frac{45}{100} = \frac{36}{100}.$$

We know that the number of blue marbles is 36. So 36 ÷ 36% = 100.

Method 2:
Let x be the number of marbles in the bag.

The number of blue marbles is $\frac{80}{100} \times (1 - \frac{35}{100} - \frac{20}{100})x$ and
$\frac{80}{100} \times (1 - \frac{35}{100} - \frac{20}{100})x = 36 \implies x = 100.$

3. **Solution:** 12.
The amount of time and the amount of wheat do not matter.
To find the average number of eggs produced per hen, we simply divide the number of eggs by the number of hens.
888 ÷ 74 = 12.

Mathcounts Chapter Competition Practice   Test 4

4. **Solution:** 32.
Container 10 has 2^{10} marbles and container 9 has 2^9 marbles. So container 5 has $2^5 = 32$ marbles.

5. **Solution:** 1.331 km.
$d = 11t^2 = 11 \times 11^2 = 11 \times 121 = 1331$ m $= 1.331$ km.

6. **Solution:** 5/2.

Method 1:
$24 = 24 \times 1 = 12 \times 2 = 8 \times 3 = 6 \times 4$.
$$\frac{1}{1} + \frac{1}{2} + \frac{1}{3} + \frac{1}{4} + \frac{1}{6} + \frac{1}{8} + \frac{1}{12} + \frac{1}{24} = \frac{24+12+8+6+4+3+2+1}{24} = \frac{60}{24} = \frac{5}{2}.$$

Method 2:
The answer is $\sigma(n)/n$, where $\sigma(n)$ is the sum of the factors of n.
$$\sigma(n) = (p_1^a + p_1^{a-1} + \ldots + p_1^0)(p_2^b + p_2^{b-1} + \ldots + p_2^0)\ldots(p_k^m + p_k^{m-1} + \ldots + p_k^0)$$

$24 = 3 \times 8 = 3 \times 2^3$

The sum of all divisors:
$$\sigma(n) = (p_1^a + p_1^{a-1} + \ldots + p_1^0)(p_2^b + p_2^{b-1} + \ldots + p_2^0)$$
$$= (3^1 + 3^0)(2^3 + 2^2 + 2^1 + 2^0) = (3+1)(8+4+2+1) = 4 \times 15 = 60$$
The answer is $60/24 = 5/2$.

7. **Solution:** 20.
Let point P be (x, y). $\lambda = AP : PB = 2 : 3$.
$$x = \frac{x_1 + \lambda x_2}{1 + \lambda} = \frac{4 + \frac{2}{3} \times 20}{1 + \frac{2}{3}} = \frac{52}{5}$$

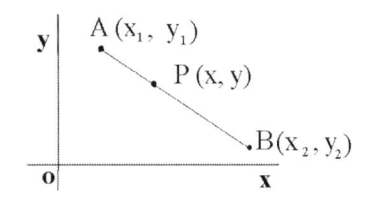

and $y = \dfrac{y_1 + \lambda y_2}{1 + \lambda} = \dfrac{12 + \frac{2}{3} \times 6}{1 + \frac{2}{3}} = \dfrac{48}{5}$. $\Rightarrow x + y = \dfrac{52}{5} + \dfrac{48}{5} = 20$.

Mathcounts Chapter Competition Practice — Test 4

8. Solution: 32.
We see that $30^3 = 27,000 < 30,000 < 40^3 = 64,000$.
So the number is larger than 30. We try $31^3 = 961 \times 31 = 29,791$.
So the answer is $31 + 1 = 32$. We check and know that 32 work: $32^3 = 1024 \times 32 = 32,768 > 30,000$.

9. Solution: 5,050.
$$1 + 2 + 3 + \ldots + 100 = \frac{(1+100) \times 100}{2} = 5050.$$

10. Solution: 60.
Method 1:
Let x be the number of balls in the bag after addition.
$$(x - 15 - 3) \times \frac{1}{2} = \frac{3}{5}x - 15 \quad \Rightarrow \quad x = 60.$$

Method 2:
Let x be the number of balls originally in the bag before addition.
Let r be the number of red balls originally in the bag before addition.

Originally: $\dfrac{r}{x} = \dfrac{1}{2} \quad \Rightarrow \quad r = \dfrac{1}{2}x \quad \Rightarrow \quad 5r = \dfrac{5}{2}x$ \quad (1)

After addition: $\dfrac{r+15}{x+15+3} = \dfrac{3}{5} \Rightarrow 5r + 75 = 3x + 45 + 9 \Rightarrow 5r + 21 = 3x$ \quad (2)

Substituting (1) into (2): $\dfrac{5}{2}x + 21 = 3x \quad \Rightarrow \quad \dfrac{1}{2}x = 21 \quad \Rightarrow \quad x = 42$

So the answer is $42 + 15 + 3 = 42 + 18 = 60$.

11. Solution: 14.
$x \# y = xy - x - y + 11 = 21 \quad \Rightarrow \quad (x - 1)(y - 1) + 10 = 21$
$\Rightarrow (x - 1)(y - 1) = 11$.
Since both x and y are positive integers, we have
  $x - 1 = 1$
  $y - 1 = 11$.
or
  $x - 1 = 11$
  $y - 1 = 1$.

In both case, $x + y = 14$.

12. Solution: 4665.

$1 + 2 + 3 + \ldots + 100 = \dfrac{(1+100) \times 100}{2} = 5050$.

$1^2 + 2^2 + 3^2 + \ldots + 10^2 = \dfrac{n(n+1)(2n+1)}{6}$.

$= \dfrac{10 \times 11 \times 21}{6} = \dfrac{2 \times 5 \times 11 \times 3 \times 7}{6} = 5 \times 11 \times 7 = 35 \times 11 = 385$.

The answer is $5050 - 385 = 4665$.

13. Solution: $3 - 2\sqrt{2}$.

$x + \dfrac{1}{x} = 6 \quad \Rightarrow \quad x^2 + 1 = 6x \quad \Rightarrow \quad x^2 - 6x + 1 = 0$.

By the quadratic formula, $x_{1,2} = \dfrac{-(-6) \pm \sqrt{(-6)^2 - 4 \times 1 \times 1}}{2} = \dfrac{6 \pm 4\sqrt{2}}{2} = 3 \pm 2\sqrt{2}$.

Since x is the smallest, $x = 3 - 2\sqrt{2}$.

14. Solution: 12.

Let g be the number of green balls and b be the number of blue balls. y be the number of balls Alex takes out.

$b + g = 25$ \hfill (1)

$y = \dfrac{b}{2} + \dfrac{g}{3} = \dfrac{b}{2} + \dfrac{25-b}{3} = \dfrac{b}{2} + \dfrac{25}{3} - \dfrac{b}{3} = \dfrac{b+50}{6}$.

Since we want the greatest value of y, we let $b = 22$ to get $y = 12$.

15. Solution: 2016π.

As shown in the figure below, point A will touch the base line again for every 3 turns ($A - A' - A''$). The distance it travels for every 3 turns is $\dfrac{2\pi r}{6} \times 4 = \dfrac{2\pi \times 6}{6} \times 4 = 8\pi$.

So after 756 turns, the distance travelled by point A is x and $\dfrac{8\pi}{3} = \dfrac{x}{756} \quad \Rightarrow \quad x = 2016\pi$

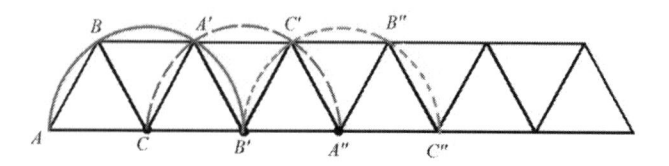

16. **Solution:** 1/21.

There are $\left\lfloor \dfrac{2016}{21} \right\rfloor = 96$ positive integer less than or equal to 2016 that are divisible by 21, where $\lfloor x \rfloor$ is called the floor function.

$P = \dfrac{96}{2016} = \dfrac{96}{21 \times 96} = \dfrac{1}{21}$.

17. **Solution:** 6.

Let x, y, and z be the numbers of 30 acres lots, 15 acres lots, and 5 acres lots, respectively.

We have the following equation: $30x + 15y + 5z = 100 \Rightarrow 6x + 3y + z = 20$.

Since the developer must have at least one lot of each type, $x, y, z > 0$.

x can only be 2, or 1.

When $x = 2$, $6x + 3y + z = 20 \Rightarrow 3y + z = 8$.
If $y = 1$, $z = 5$; if $y = 2$, $z = 2$. (Two ways).

When $x = 1$, $6x + 3y + z = 20 \Rightarrow 3y + z = 14$.
If $y = 1$, $z = 11$; if $y = 2$, $z = 8$; $y = 3$, $z = 5$; if $y = 4$, $z = 2$. (Four ways).

The solution is: 6 ways.

18. **Solution:** $2 + 2\sqrt{2}$.

By the Pythagorean Theorem, we have $a^2 + b^2 = c^2 \Rightarrow a^2 + b^2 = 4$ (1)

We are given that $\dfrac{1}{2}ab = 1 \Rightarrow 2ab = 4$ (2)

(1) + (2): $(a + b)^2 = 8 \Rightarrow a + b = 2\sqrt{2}$.

The perimeter is $2 + 2\sqrt{2}$.

19. **Solution:** 13 days.
Let d be the constant eating rate of each duck and c be the constant rate for each chicken. n be the number of days it lasts when feeding only 8 chickens.

$6(\frac{16}{d} + \frac{12}{c}) = 1 \quad \Rightarrow \quad \frac{96}{d} + \frac{72}{c} = 1$ \hfill (1)

$8(\frac{9}{d} + \frac{10}{c}) = 1 \quad \Rightarrow \quad \frac{72}{d} + \frac{80}{c} = 1$ \hfill (2)

(1) – (2): $\frac{24}{d} = \frac{8}{c} \quad \Rightarrow \quad d = 3c$ \hfill (3)

Substituting (3) into (2): $\frac{72}{3c} + \frac{80}{c} = 1 \quad \Rightarrow \quad \frac{72 + 240}{3c} = 1 \quad \Rightarrow \quad c = 104$

$n \times \frac{8}{104} = 1 \quad \Rightarrow n = 13$.

20. **Solution:** 12 cm.
Extend BA to meet CD at D.
The area of the original figure is $7^2 + 8^2 + 5^2 = 138$ cm^2.
The area of the triangle CDE is
$\frac{DE \times CD}{2} = \frac{138}{2} + 7 \quad \Rightarrow \quad \frac{(7 + AE) \times 8}{2} = 76$
$\Rightarrow \quad AE = 12$.

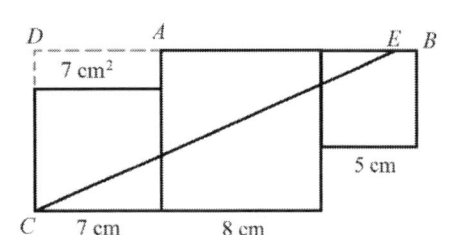

21. **Solution:** 30.
Let x be the number of marbles that must be added to make the probability of selecting a blue marble greater than 2/3.
$P = \frac{11 + x}{7 + 11 + 13 + x} > \frac{2}{3} \quad \Rightarrow \quad 3(11 + x) > 2(7 + 11 + 13 + x) \quad \Rightarrow$
$33 + 3x > 62 + 2x \Rightarrow \quad x > 62 - 33 = 29$.
The answer is 29 + 1 = 30.

22. **Solution:** 2.
The distance D traveled by the center of circle B can be used as a representative distance traveled by it.

Mathcounts Chapter Competition Practice   Test 4

$D = 2\pi(R - r) = 12\pi - 4\pi = 8\pi$.

The number of revolutions is $\dfrac{8\pi}{2\pi \times 2} = 2$

23. **Solution:** $30 + \sqrt{73}$.

If the silo were cut and spread flat, it would form a rectangular shape 8 feet wide and 21 feet high. So the length of the wire is $2AC + BD$ as shown in the figure.

$EC = 21/3.5 = 6$. $AE = \pi \times (8/\pi) = 8$.

$AC = \sqrt{AE^2 + EC^2} = \sqrt{6^2 + 8^2} = 10$.

$BD = \sqrt{DF^2 + FB^2} = \sqrt{8^2 + 3^2} = \sqrt{73}$.

The answer is $30 + \sqrt{73}$.

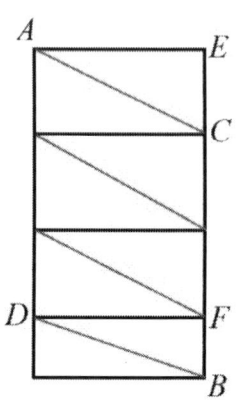

24. **Solution:** $\dfrac{17}{450}$.

We are given that the number contains one 3 (the hundreds digit).
Let the last two digits be a and b.
We have
$a + b = 0$ (00)
$a + b = 3$ (30, 03, 21, 12)
$a + b = 6$ (60, 06, 51, 15, 42, 24, 33)
$a + b = 9$ (90, 09, 81, 18, 72, 27, 63, 36, 54, 45)
$a + b = 12$ (93, 39, 84, 48, 75, 57, 66)
$a + b = 15$ (96, 69, 87, 78)
$a + b = 18$ (99)
Total: $1 + 4 + 7 + 10 + 7 + 4 + 1 = 34$.

The probability is $P = \dfrac{34}{900} = \dfrac{17}{450}$.

25. **Solution:** 2 hours.
Method 1:
Half of the time is $90 \div (9 + 6) = 6$ hours.
It takes him x hours to ride the first 45 miles, where $x = 45/9 = 5$ hours.

$y = 2 \times 6 - 5 = 7$ hours. The difference is $y - x = 7 - 5 = 2$ hours.

Method 2:
Let m be the distance travelled in first half of the time.
$$\frac{m}{9} = \frac{90-m}{6} \Rightarrow \quad \frac{m}{3} = \frac{90-m}{2} = \frac{m+90-m}{3+2} = 18 \Rightarrow \quad m = 54.$$
The time taken for Alex to ride first 45 miles is $45/9 = 5$.

The time taken for Alex to ride the second 45 miles is $(54-45)/9 + (90-54)/6 = 1 + 6 = 7$. The difference is $y - x = 7 - 5 = 2$ hours.

26. **Solution:** 24.
We see one way from E to A. We see two ways from each point B, C, or D to E. For example, we see two ways from B to E: ABE, and $ADCBE$ (see figure).
We have 6 ways from A to E.
Similarly, we have 6 ways from each of vertices D and C.
The answer is $6 \times 4 = 24$.

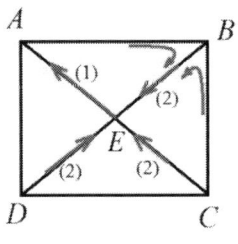

27. **Solution:** 473.
$0.\overline{3A7} = \frac{3A7}{999}$.

So $\frac{B}{1221} = \frac{3A7}{999} \quad \Rightarrow \quad \frac{B}{11} = \frac{3A7}{9} \quad \Rightarrow \quad B = \frac{3A7}{9} \times 11$.

Since B is a positive integer and 9 and 11 are relatively prime, the 3-digit number $3A7$ must be divisible by 9.

We know that A is a digit, so A must be 8. $B = \frac{387}{9} \times 11 = 43 \times 11 = 473$.

28. **Solution:** 960π.
The minute hand completes one round in every hour. The distance travelled by the tip of the minute hand in 72 hours is $72 \times 2\pi \times 7$.

The hour hand completes one round in every 12 hours. The distance travelled by the tip of the hour hand in 72 hours is $\frac{72}{12} \times 2\pi \times 4$.

The positive difference is $72 \times 2\pi \times 7 - \dfrac{72}{12} \times 2\pi \times 4 = 960\pi$.

29. **Solution:** 396.
We know that $D = 1$.

```
  ABC
+ 1EF
------
 1GB1
```

We have
Case 1: $A + 1 = 10 + G \Rightarrow A = 9 + G$. So $G = 0$ and $A = 9$.
Then we have $B + E = B \Rightarrow E = 0$ (not work because $G = 0$ already) or $1 + B + E = B$
$\Rightarrow 1 + E = 0$ (not true because E is a digit and positive).

Case 2: $1 + A + 1 = 10 + G \Rightarrow A = 8 + G$.

So if $G = 1$, $A = 9$; and if $G = 0$, $A = 8$.

For the subcase $G = 1$, $A = 9$, we have $B + E = 10 + B \Rightarrow E = 10$ (not work because E is a digit less than 10) or $1 + B + E = 10 + B \Rightarrow E = 9$ (not true because A is 9 already).
So we conclude that $G = 0$, $A = 8$.

```
  8BC
+ 1EF
------
 10B1
```

So we have
Case 1: $B + E = 10 + B \Rightarrow E = 10$ (no true since E is a digit less than 10).
Case 2: $1 + B + E = 10 + B \Rightarrow E = 9$.
Since DEF is a prim number, F can only be 3, 7, or 9 while C is 8 (not true because A is 8), 4, or 2, respectively.
So the desired number can be 197 or 199 and both are prime numbers.
So the answer is $197 + 199 = 396$.

30. **Solution:** 6.
Let the numbers be a, b, c with $a \le b \le c$.
We have $a + b + c = 12$, and $a^2 + b^2 + c^2 = 54$. Or

Mathcounts Chapter Competition Practice   **Test 4**

$a + b = 12 - c \quad \Rightarrow \quad (a+b)^2 = (12-c)^2$ (1)
$a^2 + b^2 = 54 - c^2$ (2)

Method 1:
We know that $(a-b)^2 \geq 0$ or $a^2 + b^2 \geq 2ab$ (3)
We re-write (1) as $a^2 + b^2 + 2ab = (12-c)^2$ (4)
Substituting (2) into (4): $54 - c^2 + 2ab = (12-c)^2$
$\Rightarrow 2ab = (12-c)^2 - (54-c^2)$ (5)
Substituting (2) and (5) into (3): $54 - c^2 \geq (12-c)^2 - (54-c^2)$
$\Rightarrow 2(54 - c^2) \geq (12-c)^2$.
$\Rightarrow 3c^2 - 24c + 36 \leq 0 \quad \Rightarrow \quad c^2 - 8c + 12 \leq 0 \Rightarrow (c-6)(c-2) \leq 0$.
The solution is $2 \leq c \leq 6$.
So the largest possible value for c is 6 when $a = b = 3$.

Method 2:
 By Cauchy Inequality,
$a^2 + b^2 \geq \dfrac{(a+b)^2}{2}$ (6)
Substituting (1) and (2) into (6):
$54 - c^2 \geq \dfrac{(12-c)^2}{2} \quad \Rightarrow \quad 3c^2 - 24c + 36 \leq 0 \quad \Rightarrow \quad c^2 - 8c + 12 \leq 0 \quad \Rightarrow$
$(c-6)(c-2) \leq 0$.
The solution is $\Rightarrow \quad 2 \leq c \leq 6$.
So the largest possible value for c is 6 when $a = b = 3$.

Mathcounts Chapter Competition Practice   **Test 4**

TARGET ROUND SOLUTIONS

1. **Solution:** 64.
Method 1:
Since $\angle ADE + \angle EDC = 90°$, and $\angle GDC + \angle EDC = 90°$, $\angle ADE = \angle GDC = \alpha°$. So $\angle AED = \angle GCD = \beta$.
Therefore triangle ADE is similar to triangle GDC.

$$\frac{DE}{DC} = \frac{AD}{DG} \Rightarrow \frac{10}{8} = \frac{8}{DG} \Rightarrow \frac{5}{4} = \frac{8}{DG}$$

$$DG = \frac{32}{5}.$$

$$S_{ABCD} = DG \times ED = \frac{32}{5} \times 10 = 64.$$

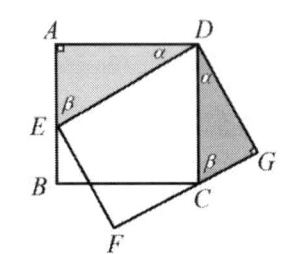

Method 2:
Connect CE.
$$S_{\triangle ECD} = \frac{1}{2} S_{ABCD}$$
$$S_{\triangle ECD} = \frac{1}{2} S_{DEFG}$$

So $S_{DEFG} = S_{ABCD} = 8 \times 8 = 64$.

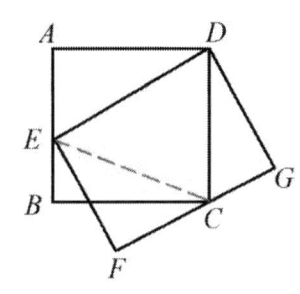

2. **Solution:** 21 km.
The truck needs to make 7 trips.
Method 1:
The distances travelled form an arithmetic sequence with first term 1000, common difference 50, and 20 terms in the sequence.

$$S = 2[a_1 + \frac{n(n-1)d}{2}] = 2[1000 + \frac{20(20-1) \times 50}{2}] = 2 \times 10500 = 21000 \text{ meters} = 21 \text{ km}.$$

Method 2:
The distance travelled for the first trip is $a_1 = 2(1000 + 50)$

Mathcounts Chapter Competition Practice   Test 4

Home
△ ——1000 m—— ☐ 50 m ☐
         Pole 1   2

The distance travelled for the second trip is $a_2 = 2(1000 + 50 \times 4)$

Home
△ ——1000 m—— ☐ 50 m ☐ 50 m ☐ 50 m ☐ 50 m ☐
         Pole 1   2   3   4   5

The distance travelled for the third trip is $a_3 = 2(1000 + 50 \times 7)$

Home
△ ——1000 m—— ☐ 50 m ☐ 50 m ☐ 50 m ☐ 50 m ☐ 50 m ☐ 50 m ☐ 50 m ☐
         Pole 1   2   3   4   5   6   7   8

Similarly, the distance travelled for the last trip is $a_7 = 2(1000 + 50 \times 19)$.
The distances travelled form an arithmetic sequence with first term $a_1 = 2(1000 + 50)$ and the last term $a_7 = 2(1000 + 50 \times 19)$, and 7 terms in the sequence.

$S = \dfrac{(a_1 + a_7) \times 7}{2} = \dfrac{2(1000+50)+2(1000+50\times 19)}{2} \times 7 = 21000$ meters = 21 km.

3. **Solution**: 43.
Let the dimension of the cube be $m = n = r = a$.
The number of cubes with two faces painted is $4(m-2) + 4(n-2) + 4(r-2)$.
So we have $4(m-2) + 4(n-2) + 4(r-2) = 492$ ⇒ $12(a-2) = 492$
⇒ $a - 2 = 41$ ⇒ $a = 43$.

4. **Solution**: 4,788.

$x^2 = 81 \times y$ (1)
$y^2 = xz$ (2)
$z^2 = 16 \times y$ (3)
We also see that $xz = 81 \times 16$ (4)

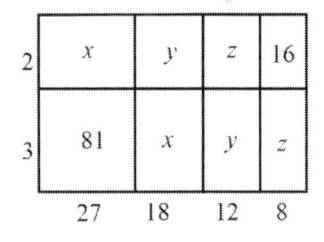

	x	y	z	16
2				
3	81	x	y	z
	27	18	12	8

Substituting (4) into (2): $y^2 = xz = 81 \times 16$ ⇒ $y = 36$.
(1) + (2) + (3): $x^2 + y^2 + z^2 = 81 \times y + xz + 16y$

103

Mathcounts Chapter Competition Practice   **Test 4**

$= 81 \times 36 + 81 \times 16 + 16 \times 36 = 4,788$.

5. **Solution:** 756.
We list a few terms to find a pattern:

Terms	1	1	2	3	5	8	13	21
Remainder	1	1	2	0	2	2	1	0

Terms	34	55	89	144	233	377	610	987
Remainder	1	1	2	0	2	2	1	0

Note that the next remainder is also found by adding up the two remainders before it. So the pattern repeats every 8 terms. In each period we get 3 terms with a remainder 2.

$2016 = 252 \times 8$. So the answer is $252 \times 3 = 756$.

6. **Solution:** 214.
We solve this problem indirectly by finding the natural numbers that do not contain the digit 4 at all.
We have the following digits available: 0, 1, 2, 3, 5, 6, 7, 8, and 9.
We have 8 one-digit numbers.
For two-digit numbers, the first digit can be 1, 2, 3, 5, 6, 7, 8, or 9. The last digit can be any of the 9 digits. So we have $8 \times 9 = 72$ two-digit numbers.

For three-digit numbers, the first digit can only be 1, 2, 3, 5, and 6. The last two digits can be any of the 9 digits.
So we have $5 \times 9 \times 9 = 405$ such three-digit numbers.

We have one more: 700.

So total we have $8 + 72 + 405 + 1 = 486$ such numbers that do not have the digit 4 at all. The answer is $700 - 486 = 214$.

7. **Solution:** 44.
Method 1:
1×1 squares: 14.
1×2 squares: $3 \times 4 + 4 = 16$.

1 × 3 squares: 2 × 4 = 8.
1 × 4 squares: 4.
2 × 2 squares: 2.
The answer is 14 + 16 + 8 + 4 + 2 = 44.

Method 2:
The number of rectangles containing the shared area *A*:
There are just three ways to pick the lower boundary and two ways to pick the top boundary. There are 3 ways to pick the right boundary and 2 ways to pick the left boundary. Their product is
$\binom{3}{1} \times \binom{2}{1} \times \binom{3}{1} \times \binom{2}{1} = 36$

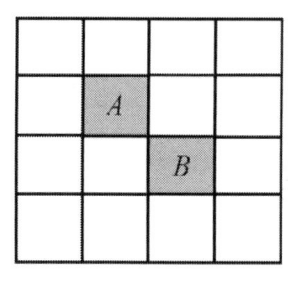

The number of rectangles containing the shared area *B*:
$\binom{2}{1} \times \binom{3}{1} \times \binom{2}{1} \times \binom{3}{1} = 36$

The number of rectangles containing the shared areas *A* and *B*:
$\binom{2}{1} \times \binom{2}{1} \times \binom{2}{1} \times \binom{2}{1} = 16$

The number of rectangles containing the shared areas *A* or *B*:
36 + 36 − 16 = 56.
The number of rectangles in the figure:
$\binom{5}{2} \times \binom{5}{2} = 100$.
The answer is 100 − 56 = 44.

8. **Solution:** $\frac{3}{2}$.

The total area of these 2016 squares is *A* and
$A = \frac{1}{1^2} + \frac{1}{2^2} + \frac{1}{3^2} + \frac{1}{4^2} + \cdots \frac{1}{2015^2} + \frac{1}{2016^2} < (1 + \frac{1}{2})^2$.

If we use a square with the side length $1 + \frac{1}{2}$, it will fit. So the answer is $\frac{3}{2}$.

Mathcounts Chapter Competition Practice   **Test 5**

MATHCOUNTS

■ **Chapter Competition** ■
Practice Test 5
Sprint Round Problems 1–30

Name _____

DO NOT BEGIN UNTIL YOU ARE INSTRUCTED TO DO SO.

This round of the competition consists of 30 problems. You will have 40 minutes to complete the problems. You are not allowed to use calculators, books or any other aids during this round. If you are wearing a calculator wrist watch, please give it to your proctor now. Calculations may be done on scratch paper. All answers must be complete, legible and simplified to lowest terms. Record only final answers in the blanks in the right-hand column of the competition booklet. If you complete the problems before time is called, use the remaining time to check your answers.

Total Correct	Scorer's Initials

Mathcounts Chapter Competition Practice   **Test 5**

1. Five identical blue boxes together weigh the same as three identical red boxes together. Each blue box weighs 6 ounces. How much do two red boxes weigh?

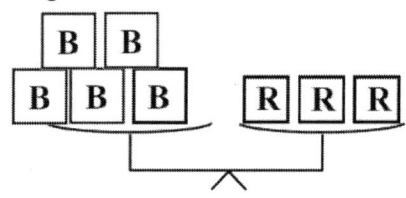

2. Find the fewest number of crickets that must hop to new locations so that each row and each column has three crickets. Crickets can jump from any square to any other square.

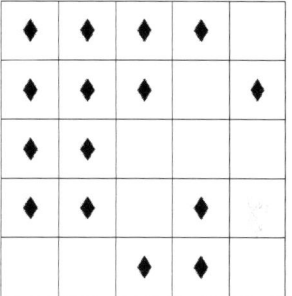

3. What is the greatest number of 1 × 1 × 2 rectangular prisms that can be placed into a rectangular box measuring 2 inches by 3 inches by 7 inches?

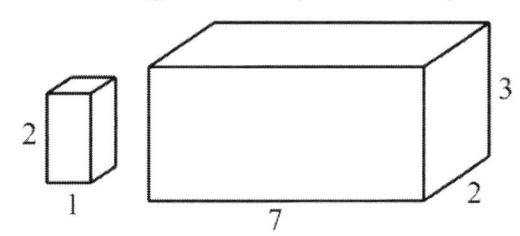

4. What fraction is equal to seven times one-eighth? Express your answer as a common fraction.

5. Krista puts 1 cent into her new bank on a Sunday morning. On Monday she puts 2 cents into her bank. On Tuesday she puts 4 cents into her bank, and she continues to double the amount of money she puts into her bank each day for two weeks. How many days will it take for the total amount of money in her bank first to exceed $20?

6. According to the table below, what is the median value of the 119 salaries paid to this company's employees?

Position Title	# of Employees with this Title	Salary for Position
President	1	$260,000
Vice-President	16	$180,000
Director	18	$150,000
Associate Director	27	$100,000
Administrative Specialist	57	$46,000

7. The diagonal AC of square $ABCD$ is tripled in length to form square $EFGH$. The perimeter of square $EFGH$ is $12\sqrt{2}$ cm. What is the area of square $ABCD$?

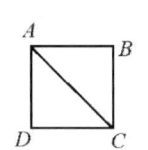

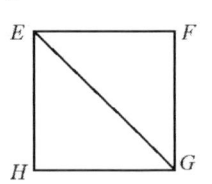

8. Boston and San Francisco are in different time zones. When it is noon in Boston it is 9 a.m. in San Francisco. A train leaves Boston at 3 p.m. (Boston local time) and arrives in San Francisco 77 hours later. What time is it in San Francisco when the train arrives?

9. A survey of 800 patients at a hospital classified the patients by gender and blood type, as shown in the table below. What percent of the patients with type B blood are male?

Mathcounts Chapter Competition Practice   Test 5

Type	A	B	O	AB	Total
Male	90	120	160	30	400
Female	110	80	200	10	400
Total	200	200	360	40	800

10. Thirty two rabbits can exchange for 4 goats. Nine goats can exchange for 3 pigs. Six pigs can exchange for 2 cows. How many rabbits can 5 cows exchange for?

11. Rick has exactly one of each of the 50 states' new U.S. quarters. The quarters were released in the same order that the states joined the union. The graph below shows the number of states that joined the union in each decade. What fraction of Rick's coins represents states that joined the union during the decades 1780 through 1849? Express your answer as a common fraction.

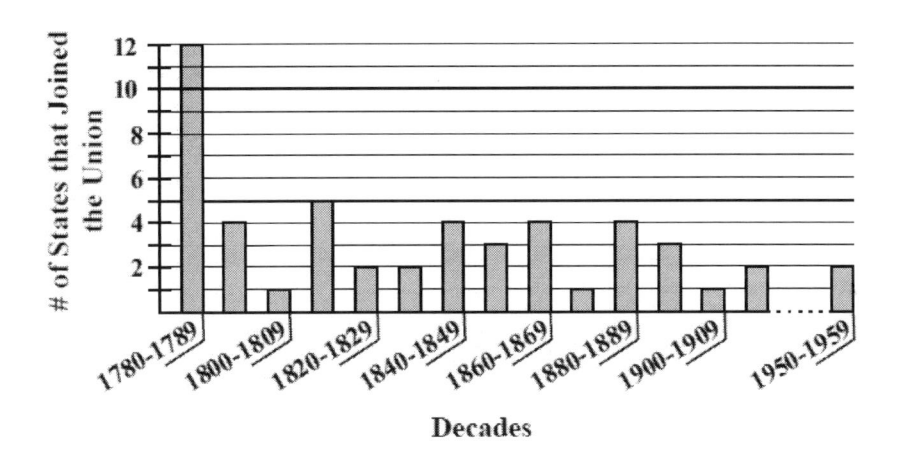

12. In the sequence 2, 3, 6, 8, 8, ..., the first term is 2 and the second term is 3. Subsequent term is the units digit of the product of the two terms before. For instance, the third term is 6, the units digit of the product $2 \times 3 = 6$; the fourth term is 8, the units digit of the product $3 \times 6 = 18$; and so on. What is the value of the 2016th term?

13. Cathy, Debra, and Emily share $2016 in a ratio of 3 : 5 : 4, respectively. How much money did Debra have?

14. To weigh things on a balance scale, one or more objects are placed on one pan and weights are placed onto the other pan until the two pans are balanced. We see A is balanced by the 4 weights shown, and B is balanced by the 5 weights shown. We have the following weights: 1, 1, 4, 4, 8, 8, 27 and 27. What is the minimum number of these weights it would take to balance the total weight of A plus B?

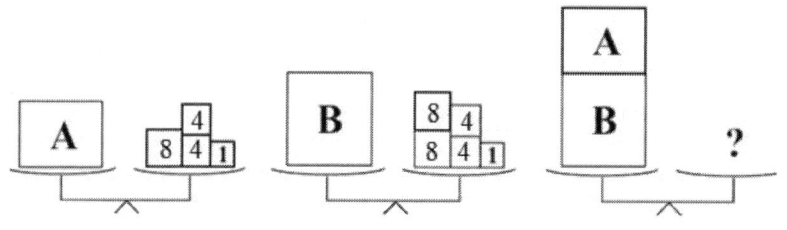

15. If $a^2 + b^2 + a^2 b^2 = 4ab - 1$, a and b are real numbers. What is the positive real value of $a + b$?

16. Each hexagon is colored either red, yellow, or blue, such that no two hexagons connected by a line segment are colored the same color. In how many different ways can the figure be colored?

Mathcounts Chapter Competition Practice — Test 5

17. *A* can run around a circular track in 70 minutes. *B*, running in the opposite direction, meets *A* every 45 minutes. What is *B*'s time to run around the track, expressed in minutes?

18. Fourteen unit cubes are glued together as shown. What is the surface area of the resulting solid?

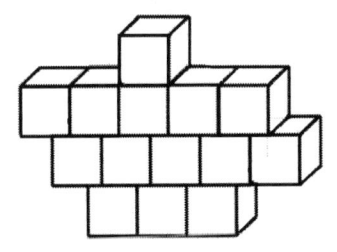

19. The graph shows the total distance Sam drove in five hours. How many miles per hour is the car's average speed for the period from 3 p.m. to 5 p.m.?

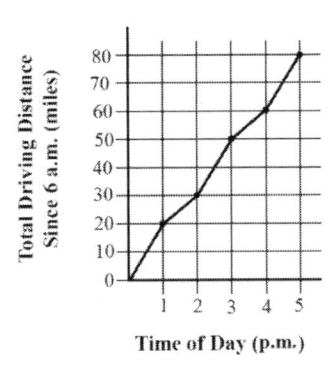

20. A stock loses 10% of its value on Monday. On Tuesday it loses 20% of the value it had at the end of the day on Monday. On Wednesday it loses 30% of the value it had at the end of the day on Tuesday. On Thursday it gains 60% of the value it had at the end of the day on Wednesday. What is the overall percent loss in value from the beginning of Monday to the end of Thursday? Express your answer as a decimal to the nearest hundredth.

Mathcounts Chapter Competition Practice Test 5

21. As shown in the figure, A, B, C, D, E, F, G, H, and I represent nine numbers from 1 to 9. The numbers in each circle is added to get a sum. The five sums form an arithmetic sequence. What is the smallest possible value of the sum of these 5 sums?

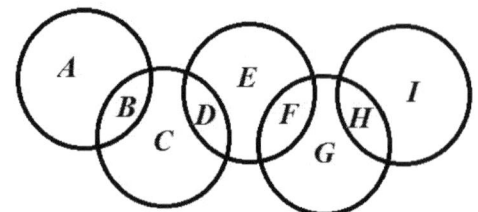

22. What is the probability that a randomly selected three-digit whole number is divisible by 3 and contains the digit 3? Express your answer as a common fraction.

23. Betsy purchased a pair of shoes for $45. Upon returning home, she discovered that the shoes were too large. Consequently, she sold the shoes to a stranger for $30. The stranger gave her a $100 bill. Betsy was not able to break the bill so she handed the bill to her friend Cathy. Cathy kept the $100 bill and gave her 10 $10 bills back. A week later, Cathy discovered that the $100 bill is fake. Betsy then paid $100 back to Cathy. What was the number of dollars has Betsy lost?

24. If 2013 is split after the third digit into a three-digit integer and a one-digit integer, then the two integers, 201 and 3, have a common factor greater than one. What is the first year other than 2016 after 2013 that has this property?

25. Two consecutive positive odd numbers are each squared. The sum of the squares is 290. What is the sum of the original two numbers?

112

Mathcounts Chapter Competition Practice — Test 5

26. What is the area of the pentagon shown here with sides of length 5, 12, 18, 12 and 13 units?

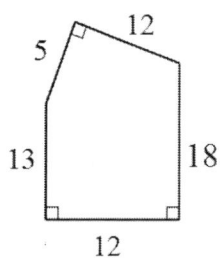

27. A job can be done by Alex alone in 6 hours and by Bob alone in 10 hours. Alex works on the job for one hour alone, then Bob continue to work on the job for one hour alone. If they repeat the pattern, in how many hours can the job be done? Express your answer as a common fraction.

28. There exist positive integers x, y, and z satisfying $28x + 30y + 31z = 365$. Compute the value of $x + y + z$.

29. Three sides of a right triangle are a, b, and c. c is the hypotenuse. a, b, and c form a geometric sequence. Find the ratio of the hypotenuse to the shorter leg. Express your answer in simplest radical form.

30. One gear turns 23 1/3 times in a minute. Another gear turns 40 times in a minute. The third gear turns 50 times in a minute. Initially, a mark on each gear is pointing due north. After how many seconds will the three gears next have their marks pointing due north?

MATHCOUNTS

■ **Chapter Competition** ■
Practice Test 5
Target Round Problems

Name _____

DO NOT BEGIN UNTIL YOU ARE INSTRUCTED TO DO SO.

This round of the competition consists of eight problems, which will be presented in pairs. Work on one pair of problems will be completed and answers will be collected before the next pair is distributed. The time limit for each pair of problems is six minutes. The first pair of problems is on the other side of this sheet. When told to do so, turn the page over and begin working. Record your final answer in the designated space on the problem sheet. All answers must be complete, legible and simplified to lowest terms. This round assumes the use of calculators, and calculations may also be done on scratch paper, but no other aids are allowed.

Total Correct	Scorer's Initials

Mathcounts Chapter Competition Practice — Test 5

1. In the maze below, a player may only move along the line segments. The number in each line segment indicates the number of hours needed to travel through the distance of the segment. What is the shortest time need to go from A to B?

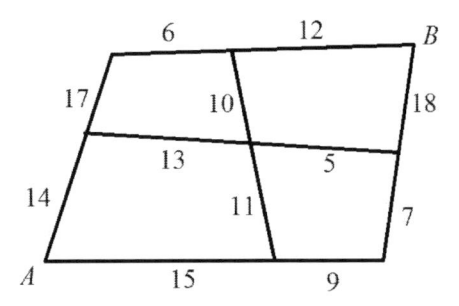

2. A cup of water is added to a container of salt water solution. The salt content (concentration) is 15% after the addition. The same amount of water is added again to the container. Now the salt content is 12% of the solution in the container. Find the original salt content of the solution in the container.

Mathcounts Chapter Competition Practice Test 5

3. How many squares are there in the figure below?

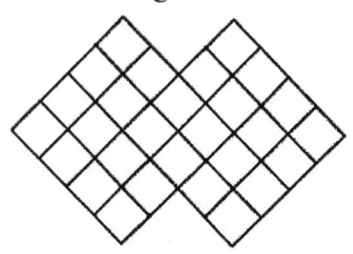

4. In the figure below, side *AE* of rectangle *ABDE* is parallel to the *x*-axis, and side *BD* contains the point *C*. The vertices of triangle *ACE* are $A(1, 1)$, $C(3, 3)$ and $E(4, 1)$. What is the ratio of the area of the shaded regions to the area of triangle *ACE*? Express your answer as a decimal to the nearest hundredth.

Mathcounts Chapter Competition Practice — Test 5

5. The geometric mean of A, B and C is 12. The value of A is four times the value of B, and the value of B is four times the value of C. What is the value of C?

6. One 5×5 grid of squares with two shaded squares is given. How many different rectangles bounded by the gridlines do not contain the shaded square?

7. A cube is labeled one of the letters of A, B, C, D, E, and F on each of its six faces. A is on the opposite side of C, B is on the opposite side of D, and E is on the opposite side of F. The cube is landing on one of the squares with the letter A. Now the cube is rolling along the edges as shown and landing on each of the twenty squares exactly once without slipping. What is the letter landing on the last square?

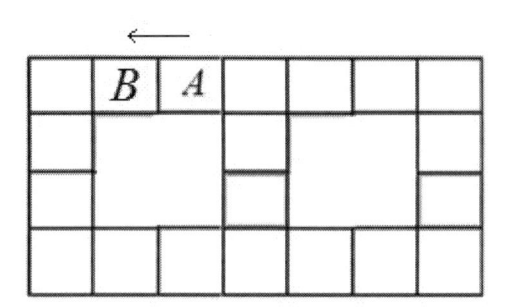

8. How many continuous paths from A to C, along segments of the figure, do not revisit any of the segments?

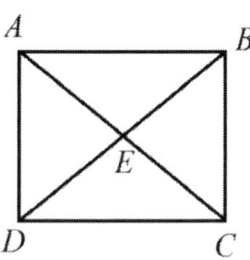

118

Mathcounts Chapter Competition Practice — Test 5

ANSWER KEYS TO TEST 5

SPRINT ROUND

1. 20.
2. 2.
3. 21.
4. $\frac{7}{8}$.
5. 11 days.
6. $100,000.

7. 2.
8. 5 p.m.
9. 60%.
10. 360.

11. 3/5.
12. 4.
13. $840.
14. 4.
15. 2.
16. 288.
17. 126 minutes.
18. 47.
19. 15.
20. 19.36%.
21. 55.
22. $\frac{7}{75}$.

23. $115.
24. 2019.
25. 24.
26. 216.
27. $\frac{22}{3}$.
28. 12.
29. $\frac{1+\sqrt{5}}{2}$.
30. 18.

TARGET ROUND

1. 48.
2. 20%.
3. 55.
4. 0.31.
5. 3.
6. 48.
7. B.
8. 19.

Mathcounts Chapter Competition Practice   **Test 5**

SPRINT ROUND SOLUTIONS

1. **Solution:** 20.
Five blue boxes weigh 6 × 5 = 30 ounces. Each red box weighs 30/3 = 10 ounces and two red boxes weigh 2 × 10 = 20 ounces.

2. **Solution:** 2.
Notice that two rows have four crickets, so at least two crickets must move. The pair of crickets at (1, 5) and (2, 4) on the main diagonal can be moved to (5, 3) and (5, 1) as shown.

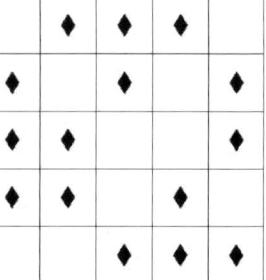

3. **Solution:** 21.
$3 \times 7 = 21$.
Or we can use the ratio of the volumes: $\dfrac{7 \times 3 \times 2}{2 \times 1 \times 1} = 21$.

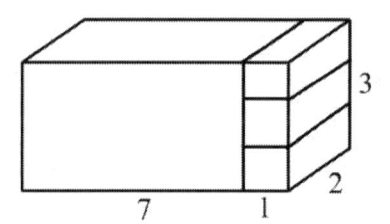

4. **Solution:** $\dfrac{7}{8}$.
$7 \times \dfrac{1}{8} = \dfrac{7}{8}$.

5. **Solution:** 11 days.
Let n be the number of days needed to have a total amount greater than $20.

$2^n - 1 \geq 2000$. We know that $2^{10} = 1024$ and $2^{11} - 1 = 2 \times 1024 - 1 = 2048 - 1 = 2047 > 2000$.
So the answer is 11.

6. **Solution:** $100,000.

The median is the middle one or number 60 (i.e., 59 + 1 + 59 = 119)

Mathcounts Chapter Competition Practice **Test 5**

Since $1 + 16 + 18 + 27 = 62$, the median is within that number, and the salary is $100,000.

7. **Solution:** 2.
The perimeter of square $EFGH$ is $12\sqrt{2}$ cm. The side length is $12\sqrt{2}/4 = 3\sqrt{2}$ cm. So the area of square $EFGH$ is $3\sqrt{2} \times 3\sqrt{2} = 18$.

$$\frac{S_{ABCD}}{S_{EFGH}} = (\frac{AC}{EG})^2 \implies S_{ABCD} = (\frac{AC}{EG})^2 S_{EFGH} = (\frac{1}{3})^2 \times 18 = 2.$$

8. **Solution:** 5 p.m.
The time difference is 3 hours between Boston and San Francisco.
$77 - 24 - 24 - 24 = 5$. Five hours after 3 p.m. is 8 p.m. So the time is 8 p.m. in Boston when the train arrives in San Francisco.
When it is 8 p.m. in Boston it is 5 p.m. in San Francisco.

9. **Solution:** 60%.
We are given a chart of male and female patients and how many have each type of blood. Since we are asked to find what percent of patients with type B blood are male, we need only consider the column dealing with type B blood.

That column shows 120 males having type B blood for a total of 200 people. So the answer is $120/200 = 60\%$.

10. **Solution:** 360.
Method 1:

Since 6 pigs can exchange for 2 cows, each cow can exchange for 3 pigs.

Three pigs can exchange for 9 goats. So 1 pig can exchange for 3 goats and 1 cow can exchange for 9 goats. Since 32 rabbits can exchange for 4 goats, 1 goat can exchange for 8 rabbits.

Five cows can exchange for 45 goats and $45 \times 8 = 360$ rabbits.

Method 2:

$32r = 4g \quad \implies \quad 8r = g \qquad\qquad (1)$

121

$9g = 3p$ (2)

$6p = 2c$ $\Rightarrow$ $3p = c$ (3)

Substituting (3) into (2): $9g = c$ $\Rightarrow 45g = 5c$ (4)

Substituting (4) into (1): $5c = 45g = 45 \times 8r = 360r$.

11. **Solution:** 3/5.
Rick has exactly one of each of the 50 states' U.S. quarters.
The graph shows that $12 + 4 + 1 + 5 + 2 + 2 + 4 = 30$ states joined the union in the decades 1780-1849. Therefore, 30/50 = 3/5.

12. **Solution:** 4.
We write the first few terms in the sequence:
2, 3, 6, 8, 8, 4, 2, 8, 6, 8, 8, 4, 2, 8, 6, 8, 8, 4, 2, 8, 6,...
The pattern is repeated after the third term: 8, 8, 4, 2, 8, 6.
$2016 = 3 + 6 \times 335 + 3$
2016th term is the same as the third term in the pattern, 4.

13. **Solution:** $840.
Debra has $\dfrac{5}{3+4+5} \times 2016 = 840$.

14. **Solution:** 4.
The weight of A and B is $(8 + 4 + 4 + 1) + (8 + 8 + 4 + 4 + 1) = 17 + 25 = 42$.

We see that $42 + 1 = 27 + 8 + 8$.

So 4 weights (1, 8, 8, 27) will do.

We also see that $42 + 8 + 4 = 27 + 27$

So 4 weights (8, 4, 27, 27) will also do. However, we are not able to get a smaller number less than 4. Thus the answer is 4.

15. **Solution:** 2.

$a^2 + b^2 + a^2b^2 = 4ab - 1$ ⇒ $(a^2 - 2ab + b^2) + (ab)^2 - 2ab + 1 = 0$ ⇒
$(a - b)^2 + (ab - 1)^2 = 0$.

Since a and b are real numbers, we have $(a - b)^2 = (ab - 1)^2 = 0$.

So $a = b$ and $ab = 1$.
$b^2 = 1$ ⇒ $a = b = 1$ or $a = b = -1$ (ignored since we want the positive value).

The answer is $1 + 1 = 2$.

16. **Solution:** 288.
Since the middle hexagons have more line segments connections, we color them first.
We have three ways to color the hexagon A (we have three colors to use to color the hexagon A), two ways to color B. If C is colored the same color as A, we have two ways to color D; If C is colored the different color from A, we have one way to color D.

So we have $3 \times 1 \times 2 + 3 \times 2 \times 2 = 6 + 12 = 18$.
We have 2 ways to color each of E, F, G, and H.
So the answer will be $18 \times 2^4 = 288$.

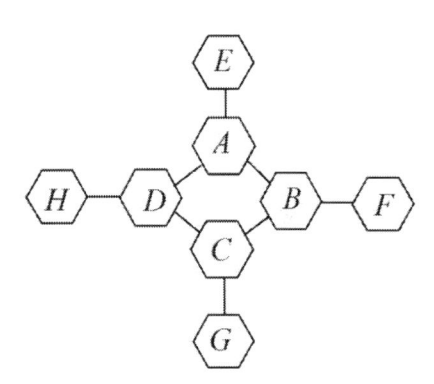

17. **Solution:** 126 minutes.
Method 1:
Let x denote B's time in minutes. Letting l represent the length of the track, we have
$\frac{1}{70}(45) + \frac{1}{x}(45) = 1$ ⇒ $x = 126$.

Method 2:
Let t be the time needed to run around the track. Then we have $\frac{45}{70 - 45} = \frac{t}{70}$.
Solving for t gives us $t = 126$ minutes.

Method 3:
Let d be the length of the path.
Since Alex can complete a circular path in 70 minutes, we have

$d = r_A t = 70 r_A$ (1)

Since they meet every 45 minutes, we have

$d = (r_A + r_B)t = 45(r_A + r_B)$ (2)

Solving (1) and (2), we get:

$r_B = \dfrac{5}{9} r_A \quad \Rightarrow \quad r_B = \dfrac{5}{9} r_A \times \dfrac{70}{70} = \dfrac{1}{126} d \Rightarrow \quad d = 126 r_B$

So it takes 126 minutes for Bob to complete the circular path.

18. **Solution:** 47.
From the top and bottom, we see 5.5 × 2 = 11 squares. From the left and right side, we see 4 × 2 = 8 squares. From the front and back, we see 14 × 2 = 28 squares.

The answer is then 11 + 8 + 28 = 47.

19. **Solution:** 15.
Sam travelled 80 – 50 = 30 miles in two hours from 3 p.m. to 5 p.m.
The average speed is 30/2 = 15 mph.

20. **Solution:** 19.36%.
Let x be the cost of the stock on Monday morning. At the end of Monday, it has lost 10% of its price or $0.1x$. So the remaining value will be $0.9x$.

At the end of the day on Thursday, the remaining value is
$1.6 \times 0.7 \times 0.8 \times 0.9 \times x = 0.8064x = (80.64\%)x$.

The overall percent loss in value from the beginning of Monday to the end of Thursday is 100% - 80.64% = 19.36%.

21. **Solution:** 55.
Five sums are: $S = (A + B) + (B + C + D) + (D + E + F) + (F + G + H) + (H + I) = (A + B + C + D + E + F + G + H + I) + (B + D + F + H) = 45 + (B + D + F + H)$

$B, D, F,$ and H count twice and other letters count once.

Since we want the smallest value of S, we let $B + D + F + H = 1 + 2 + 3 + 4 = 10$.

The answer is 45 + 10 = 55.

Mathcounts Chapter Competition Practice   Test 5

One example is

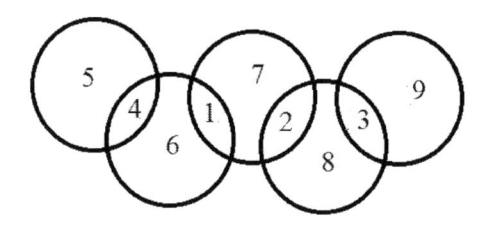

(Olympic rings diagram with numbers: 5, 4, 7, 1, 6, 2, 3, 8, 9)

22. **Solution:** $\frac{7}{75}$.

Case 1: the number contains three 3's.

We have one such number: 333   1

Case 2: the number contains two 3's.
We have
330   2
336   3
339   3

Case 3: the number contains one 3.
Let the other two digits be a and b.
We have
$a + b = 0$ (300)   1
$a + b = 3$ (~~330~~, 321)   6
$a + b = 6$ (360, 351, 342, ~~333~~)   4 + 6 + 6
$a + b = 9$ (390, 381, 372, ~~363~~, 354)   4 + 6 + 6 + 6
$a + b = 12$ (~~393~~, 384, 375, 366)   6 + 6 + 3
$a + b = 15$ (396, 387)   6 + 6
$a + b = 18$ (399)   3
Total: 1 + 2 + 3 + 3 + 1 + 6 + 16 + 22 + 15 + 12 + 3 = 84.

The probability is $P = \frac{84}{900} = \frac{7}{75}$.

23. **Solution:** $115.
Method 1:

125

Mathcounts Chapter Competition Practice   **Test 5**

Suppose the $100 bill is not fake. In the end, Betsy lost 45 − 30 = $15 only. Now the bill is fake, so she lost 15 + 100 = $115.

Method 2:
The money exchanged between Betsy and her friend Cathy does not make any difference. The only loss is due to the stranger who took away the pair of shoes ($45) and $70 change, which sum to 45 + 70 = $115.

24. **Solution:** 2019.
Consider 201 and 4. 4 is not a divisor of 201. Consider 201 and 5. 5 is not a divisor of 201. Similarly, neither 2017 not 2018 is the answer. If we move on to 2019. 201 and 9 have the common factor of 3. So 2019 will satisfy our requirements.

25. **Solution:** 24.
Let the two number be $2n + 1$ and $2n + 3$.

$$(2n+1)^2 + (2n+3)^2 = 290 \implies 8n^2 + 16n + 10 = 290 \implies$$
$$8n^2 + 16n - 280 = 0 \implies n^2 + 2n - 35 = 0 \implies (n-5)(n+7) = 0.$$

$n = 5$ and the sum of two numbers is $11 + 13 = 24$.

26. **Solution**: 216.
Method 1:
Connect BE.
ABE is a right triangle and $BCDE$ is a trapezoid.

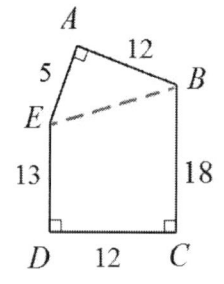

The area of the pentagon is
$$S_{\triangle ABC} + S_{BCDE} = \frac{5 \times 12}{2} + \frac{(13+18) \times 12}{2} = 30 + 186 = 216$$

Method 2:
Connect BE. Draw EF perpendicular to BC at F. $CF = DE = 13$.

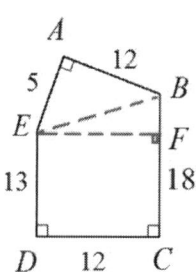

So $BF = 18 − 13 = 5$.

Both ABE and BEF are 5-12-13 right triangles and $CDEF$ is a rectangle.

126

Mathcounts Chapter Competition Practice — Test 5

The area of the pentagon is
$$2S_{\triangle ABE} + S_{CDEF} = 2 \times \frac{5 \times 12}{2} + 13 \times 12 = 60 + 156 = 216.$$

27. **Solution:** $\frac{22}{3}$.

Let the rate for Alex be $r_a = 1/6$ and the rate for Bob be $r_b = 1/10$.

The job done in every two hours is $1 \times \frac{1}{6} + 1 \times \frac{1}{10} = \frac{4}{15}$.

So the fraction part of job done is $\frac{4}{15} + \frac{4}{15} + \frac{4}{15} = \frac{12}{15} = \frac{4}{5}$ in $2 \times 3 = 6$ hours.

The job left after 6 hours of working is $1 - \frac{4}{5} = \frac{1}{5}$.

When Alex works on the job for one more hour, the job left is $\frac{1}{5} - 1 \times \frac{1}{6} = \frac{6-5}{30} = \frac{1}{30}$.

Bob needs t hour to finish the job: $t \times \frac{1}{10} = \frac{1}{30}$ $\Rightarrow$ $t = \frac{10}{30} = \frac{1}{3}$.

So the answer is $6 + 1 + \frac{1}{3} = \frac{22}{3}$ hours.

28. **Solution:** 12.

Method 1:
We notice something special about the numbers 28, 30, 31, and 365. It is a year with 28 days in February, 30 days in April, June, September, November, and 31 days in January, March, May, July, August, October, and December.
So $x = 1$, $y = 4$, and $z = 7$. $x + y + z = 12$ (months).

Method 2:
$28x + 30y + 31z = 365$.
$28(x + y + z) + y + 2z > 29(x + y + z)$
$\Rightarrow$ $365 > 28(x + y + z)$ $\Rightarrow (x + y + z) < 13.03$ \hfill (1)
$31(x + y + z) - 2x - y < 31(x + y + z)$

127

Mathcounts Chapter Competition Practice Test 5

$\Rightarrow$ $365 < 31(x+y+z) \Rightarrow (x+y+z) > 11.77$ (2)
From (1) and 2), we get $11.77 < x+y+z < 13.03$ or $12 \leq x+y+z \leq 13$
Since x, y, and z are positive integers, $x+y+z = 12$ or 13.
When $x+y+z = 13$, $28x+30y+31z = 365$ $\Rightarrow$
$28(x+y+z)+y+2z = 365 \Rightarrow$ $y+2z = 365 - 28 \times 13 = 1$ (3)
Since both y and z are positive integers, (3) has no solution.

Thus $x+y+z$ must equal 12.

29. **Solution:** $\dfrac{1+\sqrt{5}}{2}$.

Let three sides be a, b, and c. c is the hypotenuse.
We have
$a^2 + b^2 = c^2$ (1)
$\dfrac{a}{b} = \dfrac{b}{c}$ $\Rightarrow$ $b^2 = ac$ (2)
Substituting (2) into (1): $a^2 + ac = c^2$ (3)
We divide each term of (3) by a^2: $1 + \dfrac{c}{a} = (\dfrac{c}{a})^2$ (4)

Let $m = \dfrac{c}{a}$, (4) becomes: $m^2 - m - 1 = 0$

$\Rightarrow$ $m = \dfrac{-(-1) \pm \sqrt{(-1)^2 - 4 \times 1 \times (-1)}}{2} = \dfrac{1+\sqrt{5}}{2}$ ($\dfrac{1-\sqrt{5}}{2}$ ignored).

30. **Solution:** 18.

The first gear has its mark face north every $\dfrac{60}{23\frac{1}{3}} = \dfrac{60}{\frac{70}{3}} = \dfrac{18}{7}$ seconds.

The second gear has its mark face north every $\dfrac{60}{40} = \dfrac{3}{2}$ seconds.

The third gear has its mark face north every $\dfrac{60}{50} = \dfrac{6}{5}$ seconds.

We know that $[\dfrac{a}{b}, \dfrac{c}{d}] = \dfrac{ac}{gcf(ad,bc)}$. We have

Mathcounts Chapter Competition Practice   Test 5

$$[\frac{18}{7},\frac{3}{2}] = \frac{18\times 3}{gcf(18\times 2, 7\times 3)} = \frac{18\times 3}{3} = 18 \text{ seconds.}$$

$$[\frac{18}{1},\frac{6}{5}] = \frac{18\times 6}{gcf(18\times 5, 1\times 6)} = \frac{18\times 6}{6} = 18 \text{ seconds.}$$

The answer will then be: 18 seconds.

Mathcounts Chapter Competition Practice   Test 5

TARGET ROUND SOLUTIONS

1. Solution: 48.
In order to reach B, the player needs to go either through F or E.
We calculate the number of hours needed from A to F.
ADF: 37
$ADCF$: 37
$AGCF$: 36.
We calculate the number of hours needed from A to E.
AGE: 31
$AGCE$: 31
$ADCE$: 32.
Then we compare both routes:
$36 + 12 = 48$
$31 + 18 = 49$.
The answer is 48.

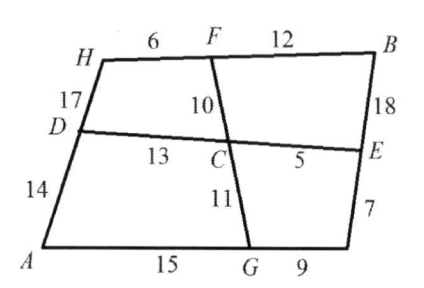

2. Solution: 20%.
Let a be the amount of salt, m be the ammount of solution, and b be the amount of water in the cup. We want to find $\frac{a}{m}$.

After the first addition, we have $\frac{a}{m+b} = \frac{15}{100}$ $\Rightarrow$ $\frac{m+b}{a} = \frac{100}{15}$

$\Rightarrow \quad \frac{m}{a} + \frac{b}{a} = \frac{20}{3} \quad \Rightarrow \quad \frac{b}{a} = \frac{20}{3} - \frac{m}{a}$ (1)

After the second addition, we have $\frac{a}{m+b+b} = \frac{12}{100}$ $\Rightarrow$ $\frac{a}{m+2b} = \frac{3}{25}$ $\Rightarrow$

$\frac{m}{a} + \frac{2b}{a} = \frac{25}{3} \quad \Rightarrow \quad \frac{2b}{a} = \frac{25}{3} - \frac{m}{a}$ (2)

(1) × 2 − (2): $0 = \frac{40}{3} - \frac{25}{3} - \frac{2m}{a} + \frac{m}{a} \Rightarrow \quad 5 = \frac{m}{a} \Rightarrow \quad \frac{a}{m} = \frac{1}{5} = 20\%$.

3. Solution: 55.
We count $4^2 + 3^2 + 2^2 + 1^2 = 30$ squares for the figure below:

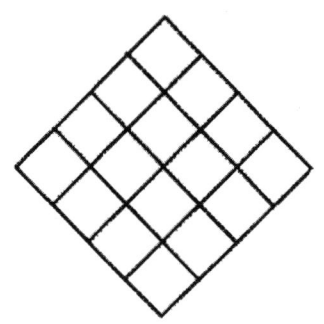

Mathcounts Chapter Competition Practice   **Test 5**

We count 5 squares belonging to both figures:

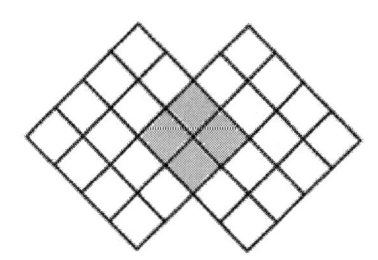

By Principle of Inclusion and Exclusion, $n = n(A) + n(B) - n(A\&B)$, we get the answer $n = 30 + 30 - 5 = 60 - 5 = 55$ squares.

4. **Solution:** 0.31.
In isosceles right triangle ABC, $AB = 2$, $BC = 2$, and $AC = 2\sqrt{2}$.
The radius of the circle is $r = \dfrac{AB + BC - AC}{2} = \dfrac{2 + 2 - 2\sqrt{2}}{2} = \dfrac{4 - 2\sqrt{2}}{2} = 2 - \sqrt{2}$.
The area of the circle is $\pi r^2 = \pi(2-\sqrt{2})^2$
The shaded area is $S_{\triangle ABC} - \pi r^2 = 2 - \pi(2-\sqrt{2})^2$.
The area of triangle $ACE = \dfrac{1}{2} S_{ABCD} = 3$.
The answer is $\dfrac{2 - \pi(2-\sqrt{2})^2}{3} = 0.31$.

5. **Solution:** 3.
Since the geometric mean of A, B and C is 12, $\sqrt[3]{ABC} = 12$.

Mathcounts Chapter Competition Practice   Test 5

Thus $ABC = 1728$ (1)

Method 1:
We factor: $ABC = 3 \times 12 \times 48$.
So $A = 48$, $B = 12$, and $C = 3$.

Method 2:
$A = 4B$ (2)
$B = 4C$ (3)
So $A = 16C$ (4)

Substituting (3) and (4) to (1): $(16C)(4C)C = 1728$ $\Rightarrow$ $C^3 = 27$ $\Rightarrow$ $C = 3$.

6. **Solution:** 48.
Method 1:
1×1 rectangle: 14.
1×2 rectangles:
We can count three 1×2 rectangles in each 1×4 rectangles:

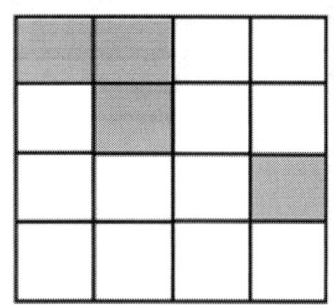

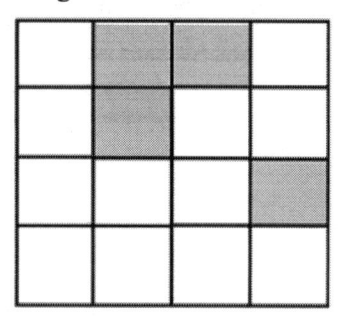

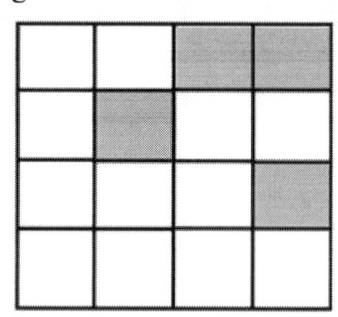

We count 5 more 1×2 rectangles as follows:

132

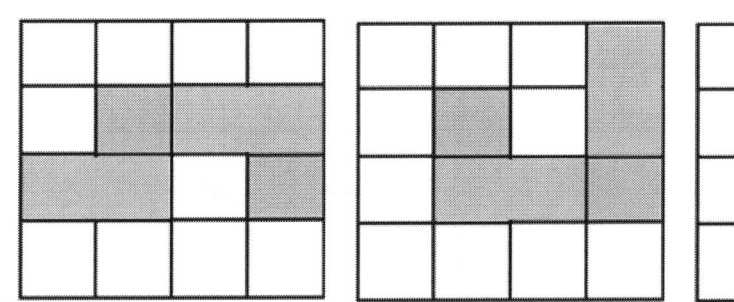

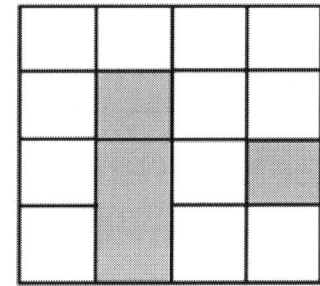

Mathcounts Chapter Competition Practice   **Test 5**

Total we have 3 × 4 + 5 = 17 1 × 2 rectangles.
Similarly we get:
1 × 3 rectangles: 2 × 4 + 1 = 9.
1 × 4 rectangles: 4.
2 × 2 rectangles: 3
2 × 3 rectangle: 1
The answer is 14 + 17 + 9 + 4 + 3 + 1 = 48.

Method 2:
The number of rectangles containing the shared area A:

There are just three ways to pick the lower boundary and two ways to pick the top boundary. There are 3 ways to pick the right boundary and 2 ways to pick the left boundary.

Their product is $\binom{3}{1} \times \binom{2}{1} \times \binom{3}{1} \times \binom{2}{1} = 36$

The number of rectangles containing the shared area B:

$\binom{2}{1} \times \binom{3}{1} \times \binom{1}{1} \times \binom{4}{1} = 24$

The number of rectangles containing the shared areas A and B:

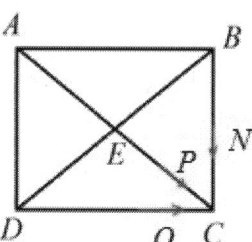

Mathcounts Chapter Competition Practice Test 5

$$\binom{2}{1} \times \binom{2}{1} \times \binom{1}{1} \times \binom{2}{1} = 8$$

The number of rectangles containing the shared areas *A* or *B*: 36 + 24 – 8 = 52.

The number of rectangles in the figure: $\binom{5}{2} \times \binom{5}{2} = 100$.

The answer is 100 – 52 = 48.

7. **Solution:** B.
We have two ways to roll the cube along the squares. The answer is *B*.

8. **Solution:** 19.
In order to reach *C*, we need to go through either *N*, *P,* or *Q*. So we divide the counting problem into three parts as follows:

Paths through *N*:
ABNC,
AEBNC,
AEDABNC,
ADEBNC,
ADEABNC.
Paths through *Q* (5 ways as well by symmetry):
ADQC,
AEDQC
AEBADQC
ABEDQC

ABEADQC

Paths through *P*:
AEPC,
AEBADEPC
AEDABEPC

ABEPC
ABEADEPC
ABEDAEPC

ADEPC
ADEABEPC
ADEBAEPC
The answer is 5 + 5 + 9 = 19.

Mathcounts Chapter Competition Practice   Index

A

absolute value, 78
arc, 62
area, 3, 6, 7, 11, 17, 21, 23, 26, 29, 35, 38, 40, 46, 50, 53, 57, 59, 62, 69, 73, 77, 83, 84, 87, 88, 97, 98, 105, 108, 113, 116, 121, 126, 127, 131, 133
arithmetic sequence, 5, 63, 102, 103, 112
average, 5, 19, 45, 46, 55, 66, 81, 92, 111, 124

B

base, 33, 50, 95

C

center, 59, 85, 97
circle, 6, 21, 62, 77, 83, 97, 112, 131
circumference, 77, 83
common factor, 112, 126
common fraction, 29, 32, 55, 56, 57, 59, 61, 63, 64, 81, 82, 84, 90, 107, 109, 112, 113, 116
congruent, 11, 26, 41, 53, 59
constant, 3
convex, 57
coordinate plane, 56
coplanar, 33
counting, 57, 134
cube, 4, 81, 88, 103, 118, 134

D

data, 29, 41
decimal, 9, 30, 67, 81, 111
degree, 33
degree measure, 33
diagonal, 38, 108, 120
diameter, 21, 77, 84
difference, 4, 17, 29, 31, 44, 56, 63, 82, 85, 99, 100, 102, 121
digit, 4, 5, 18, 20, 30, 31, 33, 40, 44, 55, 56, 58, 66, 67, 72, 73, 76, 84, 85, 89, 98, 99, 100, 104, 109, 112
dividend, 24
divisible, 5, 14, 20, 29, 31, 37, 40, 44, 55, 66, 82, 84, 96, 99, 112
divisor, 126

E

edge, 2, 31, 107
endpoint, 64
equation, 41, 42, 96
equilateral, 56, 68, 82
equilateral triangle, 56, 68, 82
even number, 64, 79
expression, 3, 57

F

face, 46, 85, 88, 128
factor, 11, 24, 25, 26, 58, 132
formula, 16, 17, 21, 49, 50, 69, 77, 81, 95
fraction, 15, 31, 56, 107, 109, 127
function, 6, 96

G

geometric mean, 117, 131
geometric sequence, 31, 42, 113
graph, 32, 109, 111, 122

H

hexagon, 2, 14, 26, 31, 33, 38, 43, 53, 56, 59, 68, 110, 123
hypotenuse, 83, 113, 128

I

inequality, 67, 68
integer, 4, 9, 19, 20, 26, 29, 31, 32, 35, 36, 40, 42, 45, 51, 56, 58, 68, 81, 82, 84, 96, 99, 112
integers, 3, 4, 5, 9, 10, 14, 29, 32, 35, 40, 50, 57, 58, 71, 73, 82, 94, 112, 113, 128
isosceles, 131

Mathcounts Chapter Competition Practice — Index

L

least common multiple, 52
line, 4, 19, 30, 41, 50, 56, 64, 68, 79, 82, 95, 110, 115, 123
line segment, 19, 50, 64, 79, 110, 115, 123
lowest terms, 1, 8, 28, 34, 54, 60, 80, 86, 106, 114

M

median, 108, 120, 121
midpoint, 4, 19
mixed number, 57
multiple, 20, 32, 46, 47, 52, 55, 66

N

natural number, 37, 89, 104
natural numbers, 37, 89, 104
negative number, 82
numerator, 31

O

odd number, 11, 26, 79, 112
opposites, 118
ordered pair, 4

P

parallel, 116
parallelogram, 26, 33, 35, 48, 98
pentagon, 33, 113, 126, 127
percent, 2, 14, 108, 111, 121, 124
perimeter, 35, 50, 83, 97, 108, 121
perpendicular, 126
point, 9, 21, 30, 38, 57, 62, 77, 81, 82, 93, 95, 116
polygon, 31, 43
polynomial, 56
prime number, 40, 70, 100
prism, 56
probability, 29, 40, 55, 59, 61, 64, 66, 74, 76, 82, 83, 84, 97, 98, 112, 125
product, 3, 6, 22, 29, 30, 33, 40, 55, 63, 64, 79, 105, 109, 133
proper fraction, 9
pyramid, 33

Pythagorean Theorem, 41, 96

Q

quadrilateral, 3, 7, 23, 57, 69

R

radius, 21, 77, 131
random, 32, 55, 64
rate, 3, 84, 97, 127
ratio, 3, 4, 17, 18, 36, 56, 68, 81, 110, 113, 116, 120
real number, 6, 33, 47, 85, 110, 123
real numbers, 6, 33, 47, 85, 110, 123
reciprocal, 82
rectangle, 6, 7, 23, 62, 69, 77, 87, 88, 116, 126, 132, 133
relatively prime, 20, 99
remainder, 66, 89, 104
repeating decimal, 84
right triangle, 40, 43, 49, 69, 77, 83, 113, 126, 131

S

sequence, 5, 30, 41, 89, 102, 103, 109, 122
set, 37, 64
similar, 102
solution, 51, 52, 85, 96, 101, 115, 128, 130
square, 4, 6, 22, 23, 29, 33, 35, 37, 38, 55, 57, 66, 70, 82, 84, 87, 90, 105, 107, 108, 117, 118, 121
sum, 3, 4, 5, 9, 10, 11, 15, 20, 24, 26, 29, 30, 32, 33, 35, 36, 44, 45, 50, 51, 57, 58, 63, 70, 72, 78, 81, 82, 85, 93, 112, 126
surface area, 56, 68, 111

T

term, 21, 30, 41, 102, 103, 109, 122, 128
tetrahedron, 58, 72
trapezoid, 46, 126
triangle, 4, 11, 26, 29, 38, 40, 56, 68, 77, 82, 83, 97, 102, 116, 131

U

union, 109, 122
unit fraction, 31, 44

Mathcounts Chapter Competition Practice — Index

unit price, 71

V

vertex, 2, 14, 31, 35, 37, 43, 48, 87
volume, 33, 49, 51, 56, 58, 68, 72

W

whole number, 5, 11, 26, 84, 112
whole numbers, 5

X

x-axis, 116

Z

zero, 36, 50, 51

Made in the USA
Middletown, DE
04 September 2018